DON'T FORGET YOUR FREE BOOKS

D0104468

HOW TO SURVIVE A FREAKIN' BEAR ATTACK

...AND 127 OTHER SURVIVAL HACKS YOU'LL HOPEFULLY NEVER NEED

BILL O'NEILL

ISBN: 978-1-64845-091-4

CONTENTS

Disclaimer 1

Introduction 2

1. How to survive a bear attack 5

2. How to survive a lightning strike 8

3. How to survive a night on a mountain 10

4. How to find a lost person 12

5. How to escape being buried alive 14

6. How to make a torch 16

7. Top five survival hacks: soda bottle 17

8. How to survive falling over a waterfall 19

9. How to extinguish a fire 21

10. How to build a fire 23

11. How to escape a sinking vehicle 26

12. How to make a makeshift sailboat 28

13. How to cross a river 30

14. How to fix a broken bone 32

15. How to know if a plant is edible 34

16. How to build a rope bridge 36

17. How to make an axe...37

18. How to tell if someone is lying 39

19. How to survive eating something you shouldn't.................41

20. How to survive a run-in with a swarm of bees.......................43

21. How to survive a heart attack 45

22. How to escape from a locked room...........................46

23. How to tell if an animal is venomous 48

24. Top five survival hacks: sticky tape...........................50

25. How to make a tourniquet...52

26. How to survive a snake attack.................................54

27. How to make a life preserver 56

28. How to walk without being heard............................57

29. How to survive a plane crash.....................................58

30. How to survive a meteor strike 60

31. How to perform a tracheotomy.................................62

32. How to survive falling through ice............................64

33. How to open a stuck jar...66

34. How to survive a crocodile attack..............................67

35. How to live in antarctica 69

36. How to escape a burning building 71

37. How to gut and clean a fish......................................73

38. How to deal with a panic attack................................74

39. How to make a bow and arrow..................................76

40. How to find water in the desert..78

41. How to hotwire a car engine 80

42. How to stitch a wound..81

43. How to survive a night in the desert 83

44. How to survive a flash flood 85

45. How not to be your own worst enemy 86

46. How to sew..87

47. How to find fresh water...88

48. How to preserve food...90

49. How to survive in a cave..91

50. How to win a fist fight 93

51. How to climb a tree..95

52. How to treat an animal bite 97

53. How to make a slingshot..98

54. How to build a makeshift canoe 100

55. How to start a fire with a battery..102

56. How to treat a burn..103

57. How to fix a puncture 104

58. How to open handcuffs 105

59. How to escape from the trunk of a car 106

60. How to survive a tornado 107

61. Top 5 survival hacks: dental floss..109

62. How to use stones to heat your home 111

63. How to make a compass 112

64. How to catch a fish 113

65. How to tie a knot..115

66. How to survive an avalance 117

67. How to treat a gunshot wound 119

68. How to restart a heart 121

69. Top five survival hacks: mobile phone 123

70. How to survive being lost at sea 125

71. How to stop a car with no brakes 127

72. How to open a can without a can opener....................129

73. How to survive losing a limb.......................................131

74. How to crack a safe...133

75. How to escape from zip ties 135

76. How to survive a spider bite 136

77. How to remove your own appendix.............................137

78. How to survive an earthquake 139

79. How to survive a tsunami 140

80. How to free yourself from a straitjacket 142

81. How to build a shelter 144

82. How to dry out wood for burning...............................146

83. How to escape an upside-down vehicle.......................148

84. How to boost your phone signal 149

85. How to find which way is north 150

86. How to navigate using the stars 151

87. How to light a wet match 152

88. How to escape a rip current..153

89. How to treat sunburn 154

90. How to escape from quicksand 155

91. How to make a whistle 157

92. How to read a map 158

93. How to boat down rapids 160

94. How to sharpen a knife...161

95. How to safely transport fuel 162

96. How to sterilize a wound 163

97. Top five survival hacks: signal for help 164

98. How to make a rope swing..166

99. How to survive a long fall...167

100. How to pick a lock 169

101. How to start a fire...171

102. How to get honey from a beehive 172

103. How to make saltwater drinkable..173

104. How to make a fire in snow 174

105. How to make a sling...175

106. How to repair a sail..176

107. How to escape being hunted by an animal...........................177

108. How to smash a window 179

109. How to survive in a falling elevator 180

110. How to survive on a desert island 181

111. How to preserve meat in the wild 183

112. How to stop a runaway train 184

113. How to find a suitable campsite 185

114. How to make your own rope 186

115. How to light a flare 188

116. How to clean dirty water 189

117. How to land a plane 190

118. How to survive a wolf attack 192

119. How to treat a snake bite 193

120. How to survive a shark attack 195

121. How to find your way out of a forest 197

122. How to build a makeshift weapon 199

123. How to see off a charging animal 200

124. How to survive a shipwreck 201

125. How to break down a door 202

126. How to survive a wildfire 203

127. How to find food in the wild 205

128. How to survive a snowstorm 206

Conclusion 208

DISCLAIMER

This book is primarily intended for entertainment and popular interest purposes only. Although every effort has been made to ensure the advice and guidelines presented in this book are accurate, these explanations are light-hearted and cursory, and should not replace the formal advice and instructions of survival experts and those with professional experience in the subjects and situations discussed here. The advice and lifehacks that follow should not be attempted without further research and without taking on board the specialist knowledge of genuine experts in these fields. This is a book intended to help you stay safe - so always prioritize your own safety!

INTRODUCTION

Here's a story to get us started.

Once upon a time, an old lady lived alone in a rural area of India, with no one to keep her company except her lovable pet bear. The bear had been orphaned as a cub, and the lady had raised him ever since on a diet of bottled milk, fish, and homegrown fruits and vegetables.

Ordinarily, the bear was free to roam the land around her home, but at night - and every Sunday, when the lady left to visit her sister in the neighboring village - she kept him on a leash in the corner of his paddock. One weekend, she did precisely that, and fastened the bear as usual to the post in the corner of his field and set off walking down the long rubbly road to her sister's home in the next village.

A few hundred yards from her house, however, she heard a sound behind her and turned to see her bear slowly following her along the road.

"How did you get out?" She exclaimed angrily. "Have you broken your leash?"

The bear continued happily ambling its way toward her.

"No!" She continued. "You know the rules. Whenever I visit my sister, you have to stay behind!" She walked up to the bear and gave it a chastising knock on its muzzle with her umbrella. "Now, turn around, and go home!"

The bear snorted gently, and having given the woman a curious look, turned and began lumbering its way back down the path toward the house. Having watched it leave, the woman continued on her way.

A few hours later, she returned home expecting to find her bear running wild around its paddock, having presumably slipped or broken its leash. What she found instead was her tame bear still tied up, sleeping soundly in the afternoon sunshine, waiting patiently for her to return, as it did every weekend.

That could only mean one thing: the bear she had encountered on the road - and which she had casually seen off with nothing more than her umbrella and her self-confidence - was a fully grown *wild* bear.

It's a story almost too extraordinary to believe, yet it's popularly claimed to be true: an old woman once saw off a bear with nothing more than an umbrella.

That's certainly one way to survive a run-in with a wild animal, of course, but what if you haven't got a trusty umbrella at hand? What then?

And what if it's not a bear that is staring you down but a pack of wolves? Or a shark? Or a venomous snake? And how would you even know if the snake across your path was venomous or not? What then?

The big wide world is a minefield of potential run-ins like these. So how would you survive? What follows provides the answer.

This book is a how-to guide for surviving not just a bear attack, but 127 other extraordinary situations - from landing a plane to escaping from the trunk of a car. How would you survive on a desert island? How can you make saltwater drinkable? How can you make a rope, escape from quicksand, or survive a plummeting elevator?

How likely are you ever to need any of these skills? It's impossible to tell - at least, that is, until the day you find yourself on a rural road, face to face with a bear, with not even an umbrella to help you...

1.

HOW TO SURVIVE
A BEAR ATTACK

Admittedly, bear attacks are rare. Bears only tend to become violent when food is scarce or when they have cubs to protect. Even so, though bears are naturally curious creatures - and so might well be drawn toward investigating anything or anyone new that wanders into their territory - they seldom escalate chance encounters like these into full-blown attacks. And even if a bear somewhat intimidatingly rises onto its hind legs, it's probably just trying to get a better look at you and find out what you are; this is by no means a sign that it is going to attack.

If a bear has got its eye on you, however, you should make it just as clear to the bear that *you* have noticed *it*. Talking and waving your arms above your head will help to signal to the bear that you are human - that is to say, not its typical prey animal. Conversely, any high-pitched screaming or crying might inadvertently make you sound like an injured animal. Best keep any outbursts like those to a minimum.

Do not run, and do not climb a tree, as bears are perfectly capable of following you up into the tree. Instead, move slowly to higher ground, as it can give the illusion that you're larger than you truly are. If that's not an option, your best bet is to remain in place and hold your ground. If a bear sees you as just as intimidating a challenge as you see it, it will be much less likely to risk investigating you further.

What happens next depends on the bear. With grizzlies and brown bears, lie on your front with your legs slightly apart, to make it harder for the bear to turn you over. Your backpack (if you have one) will give you some protection to your back but hold your hands tight together over the back of your neck to protect it too. Play dead as best you can to deter the bear from continuing – but if the attack persists, you should fight back with whatever you have at hand. Target your kicks and blows on the bear's head and face, so it knows you're a force to be reckoned with and understands the attack is not worth maintaining.

With black bears, the opposite holds true. If the bear charges or attacks, do not play dead but make yourself as intimidating as possible. Move quickly to a place of safety, like a vehicle or building, but if that's not an option, fight back with anything you can, targeting the bear's sensitive face, snout, and muzzle.

As rare as bear attacks like these are, of course, your best bet to surviving an encounter with a bear is not to encounter one in the first place. If you're a hiker, follow the rules and advice of your local park, whose rangers will know the local wildlife better than anyone and which areas are safest or to be avoided.

2.

HOW TO SURVIVE
A LIGHTNING STRIKE

You've doubtless been caught outside during a thunderstorm before, and you've perhaps heard that you should seek shelter under a tree to avoid being struck by lightning. But that is little more than an old wives' tale - and a dangerous one at that.

In fact, according to the National Weather Service, sheltering under a tree during a storm is one of the leading causes of injuries relating to lightning strikes. So, if there's a storm brewing, what is the best course of action to ensure you remain safe?

Understandably, heading indoors is your safest bet, but if you're outside then a vehicle will work as an excellent shelter too; if a car is struck by lightning, its metal chassis will conduct the electricity around you, like a Faraday cage, and safely discharge it into the earth. If you're caught well and truly out in the open, however, your best option is to find a relatively low spot - like a ditch or even a bunker on a golf course - and crouch down, keeping as low to the ground as possible, with your hands held over the back of your head.

Some people have reported bizarre phenomena before a lightning strike, so if you begin to hear a crackling or buzzing in the air, feel a tingling or goosebump-like sensation on your skin, or even see a faint bluish haze around any nearby metallic objects, there is a good chance a strike is imminent. Seek shelter or hunker down and wait for the storm to pass.

3.

HOW TO SURVIVE A NIGHT ON A MOUNTAIN

So, you've gone hiking, but the weather has closed in and you have no way of climbing back down to safety. With night fast approaching and the temperature dropping, it's becoming clear that you're going to have to spend the night on the mountainside. So, what to do?

If you'd planned ahead of time to camp out in the mountains, you will likely be well furnished with blankets, waterproofs, torches, stoves, and plenty of food and fresh water - in which case your only issue would be in finding a safe spot to bed down for the night and prepare your supper. Spending an unexpected night in the mountains is a different challenge, however, and you could easily find yourself stuck thousands of feet in the air with little more than shorts and a t-shirt.

Your main problem here will be escaping the elements. If you're not appropriately dressed, the wind and the rain can be a lot more dangerous than the dark, so seek out somewhere that keeps you as sheltered as possible.

No matter how keen to get home you are, if you're hungry, dehydrated, or exhausted, attempting to continue down the mountainside is a bad idea. Mistakes can easily be made, and if you're feeling woozy or lightheaded, you're much more likely to stumble or misstep, especially in the dark.

If there is a group of you, stay close, huddle together and most importantly stay together. Never underestimate how much your body heat can help to keep you and others warm. If you're able to, make a fire. It can provide much-needed light as well as heat and can act as a beacon if visibility is good.

If you're only stranded for a night, dehydration is a more pressing concern than hunger, so finding a source of fresh water is important. Mountain springs and melting snow are good options, but if the water looks unclean, don't risk it - it's much easier to see out a few hours with limited water than deal with a stomach bug halfway up a mountain.

If you're able to find your way back down the following morning, do so safely. But if not, awaiting rescue is your best option, in which case stay where you are. How will anyone know to come and rescue you? Well, that's where rule number one comes in: before you even head off into the mountains, always let someone know where you're going, what route you expect to take, and how long you expect to be there.

4.

HOW TO FIND
A LOST PERSON

Thanks to social media, nowadays it can seem impossible *not* to know what everyone is up to 24/7. But what if someone does really drop off the map and disappear? How can you find a lost person?

Admittedly, that's an impossibly broad question. Finding a long-lost relative or getting in touch with an old friend is different from finding a hiker lost in the woods, which is different again from locating a child lost in a shopping mall.

In looking for an old friend and or a distant cousin, the search often has to begin online - sifting through census records, social media profiles, telephone directories, and so on. But simply finding someone who lives in another town is hardly a survival situation. What if the search is a little more life-or-death?

The technologies involved in finding someone lost in the wilderness have advanced enormously in the past few decades, with previous feet-on-the-ground searches now supplemented by search-and-rescue aircraft observations, reams of GPS data, and mobile phone forensics. Of these, tracking cell phone signals are now among the most important methods of finding a lost person, with technicians capable of translating the data from signal towers into three-dimensional geographic pictures, giving a trail of phone-signal breadcrumbs showing a person's recent whereabouts.

Where phone signals vanish, however, things become trickier. Most modern mobile telephones still contain GPS trackers, but once batteries die and signals dwindle, they're not of much use.

Contact the local police department and provide them with an accurate description of the missing person. What were they wearing on the day they went missing? Did they tell you where they were going or what walking route they were taking? Not only that, but how fast do they tend to walk when they're in the great outdoors? Do they have any medical conditions or injuries? How experienced are they concerning outdoor life?

Any feet-on-the-ground searches should then involve as many people as possible, in one long line so that as much ground as possible can be covered together. Any clues can be meaningful at this stage - from dropped bottle caps and ring-pulls to footprints, handprints, and even blood stains. From there, it's only a matter of time.

5.

HOW TO ESCAPE BEING BURIED ALIVE

Admittedly, this isn't among the most likely of scenarios, but it's been the plot of enough horror movies and TV episodes to make it a question worth asking. How can you escape if you've been buried alive?

Let's first limit the field to the standard procedure: you're in a coffin, five or six feet below the ground. Apart from how in the heck you managed to get yourself into such a situation, your first concern is not escaping but your air supply.

A typical person will use up all the fresh air in a standard coffin-sized box within only a few hours. You have no chance of escaping at all if you've suffocated, so keep your breathing as slow and calm as possible (given the circumstances, obviously), as hyperventilating will only use up what little air you have faster.

To get out, you're going to need to break the timber of the coffin. Luckily, there's a fair chance the coffin lid will have broken or buckled under the weight of the soil above, so feel for any splits or weak points that might already be there. Use your legs to kick against any weaknesses in the timber, as you'll be able to get more force behind them than your hands and arms alone.

As the wood breaks, the earth above it will naturally fall away. It will likely still be fairly loose, so you should be able to manipulate it away from you as it falls. Push as much of it as you can down to the empty space at your feet. Use your clothes to cover your mouth and nose.

As more of the earth and timbers give way, use the looseness of the earth to your advantage and push against it to haul yourself upward into a seat position. As more earth falls in beneath you, continue pushing upward, getting as much of the soil below your body to give you a height advantage. Continue pushing upward - think of swimming to the surface of a swimming pool - gradually shifting from a seated to a standing position. Eventually, you should be able to push aside enough of the remaining loose earth around you to break the surface.

6.

HOW TO MAKE
A TORCH

A flaming torch is essentially a wax less candle. In other words, to make one, you need a wick and some kind of fuel.

Long strips of fabric work perfectly, so tear away at your shirt sleeve and wrap it snugly around the end of a pole or branch. The branch needs to be long enough to hold the burning tip far from your face, and wide and sturdy enough not to snap or droop with the weight. If you don't have fabric to hand (or aren't too keen to tear your clothes to pieces), strips of birch bark will make a suitable replacement.

The wick needs fuel to burn properly. After all, when you light a candle, it's the wax that fuels the flame, not the string of the wick. Soak the fabric or bark-covered tip in some kind of flammable liquid - the fluid from a cigarette lighter, campsite kerosene, or even rendered animal fat will all work well.

To light the wick, hold the torch upright, making sure none of your fuel drips onto your hands, and then hold a flame to the bottom of it. It may take a moment to catch, so be patient. Once alight, the torch should burn for 30 minutes or so.

7.

TOP FIVE SURVIVAL HACKS: SODA BOTTLE

Here are some hints and tips to show how a humble plastic water bottle might be one of the most valuable items you take with you into the great outdoors.

1. **MAKE A ROPE.** The plastic used to make soda bottles is surprisingly strong. Cut off the base of the bottle and use a sharp knife—and a lot of patience—to trim away a long coiling filament from the round edge. The result will be a remarkably durable and entirely waterproof string or cord.

2. **MAKE A WATER PURIFIER.** So long as your bottle still has its cap, you can use it to make a perfectly usable water distiller. Cut off the bottom and curl or fold the end inward to make a lip. Fasten the cap onto the bottle and place it over the water you want to purify. You can do this either by balancing the bottle on rocks or sticks above a muddy puddle or else fill a smaller container like a drink can and place that inside. Then place the entire contraption in the sun. As the air inside the bottle heats up, clean water will evaporate from the liquid and condense against the inside of the bottle, from where it will trickle down into the folded lip to be collected.

3. **MAKE A FISH TRAP.** Cut the top of the bottle, then push it securely back inside the bottle the opposite way around - so the top sits inside the bottle itself. Secure the top, either with glue or tape or by piercing through both layers of plastic with a sharp twig and tying them together with string or strong grass. If you can, place some kind of foodstuff inside the main body of the bottle, then submerge the entire device in a river, lake, or body of water. Small fish attracted by the bait will swim into the tapering bottle top but find it difficult to work their way back out.

4. **KEEP YOUR PACK AFLOAT.** Need to cross a river? A large plastic bottle might not quite have the buoyancy required to help you stay afloat but tying it to smaller items like your backpack can help to keep them bobbing along on the surface as you wade or swim your way across.

5. **FASHION A SPLINT**. The shape formed by cutting a bottle lengthways, from cap to base, can be used for everything from a makeshift spade to a rainwater catcher. In desperate circumstances, cutting a U-shaped trough out of a plastic bottle can even make a splint for supporting an injured arm.

8.

HOW TO SURVIVE FALLING OVER A WATERFALL

Let's be honest here: this one very much depends on the waterfall.

If you're unlucky enough to find yourself tumbling over a fast-flowing series of rapids, your best bet is to adopt what is known as the passive swimming position - a loose-limbed, feet-first posture that allows you to push away from any rocks you catch with your feet. Tumbling feet first also lowers the risk of a flailing arm becoming trapped on an underwater obstacle. As the current slackens, you can try swimming ashore, or else wait until it slows entirely and drift to the water's edge.

Surviving a plunge down a single tall waterfall, however, is a different beast altogether. To survive the fall at all, you'll need sufficient room in the plunge pool - the trough of water into which it empties - to absorb your dive. So long as the geography of the waterfall itself is suitable, to survive you'll still need to take a deep breath as you go over the edge - sufficient air to see you through the fall and the rise to the surface of the pool below.

Try to position yourself so you fall feet first, keeping your body tense and your legs together. Close your eyes and mouth and hold your arm over your face so that your nose is nestled in the crook of your elbow. That will not only stop water from swilling into your nose when you land but also help to protect it from any rocks or debris.

The water thundering down around you will pack a punch and could be filled with debris, so as soon as you splash down, begin to swim away toward the shore. After all, you don't want to survive the fall only to be concussed by a torrent of water or the bough of a fallen tree.

9.

HOW TO EXTINGUISH
A FIRE

There's a simple reason why fire extinguishers come in different colors and sizes: not all fires are the same.

Putting out a grease fire is different from putting out an electrical fire while extinguishing a burning pan in the kitchen (by draping a saturated towel over it) is a very different task to putting out that potential inferno you've started by foolishly lighting a disposable barbecue in the middle of a drought-ridden field.

No matter how they are started, however, all fires can be put out in one of four ways: cooling, smothering, starving, or interrupting.

Cooling involves limiting the temperature of the fire and its fuel, by increasing the rate at which heat is lost from the burning material. So, when you pour water on a fire, one of the immediate effects it has is to disrupt the heat balance of the fire - lowering the temperature of the fuel to a point at which it is not sufficient to continue burning.

Smothering involves depriving the fire of the oxygen it needs to burn - more specifically at the seat of the fire, where the combustion process itself takes place. It's this principle that works when a candle is snuffed out. It's also the principle behind fire blankets, which quash the flames through their sheer weight and denseness.

Starving the fire involves limiting or depriving it of the fuel itself. As counterintuitive as it may seem, forest fires, for instance, can be stopped in their tracks by pulling down trees or even scorching the earth around them so that there is nothing left to burn.

Interrupting the combustion process is the trickiest and least obvious way of putting out a fire, but there's no denying how it works. Dry powders - most notably, a substance called bromochlorodifluoromethane, or BCF - work to interrupt the reaction that causes the combustion of burning materials, and thereby stop a fire chemically. It is dangerous to breathe this chemical so remove yourself from the area as quickly as possible.

10.

HOW TO
BUILD A FIRE

Pre-cut packs of firewood come with a handy set of instructions to piece together a fire in a grate safely and quickly. But what if you're out in the wilderness with no such store to choose from, and it's up to you to source what you need and build the fire from scratch?

First things first, you'll need to source your raw materials - stones, firewood, kindling, and tinder - and find a suitable spot away from overhanging trees and bushes.

Clear the ground of any dry leaves and grasses, then arrange the stones in a circle. These will stop the fire from spreading. If the ground is damp, you'll have to build the fire on top of a bed of rocks, so fill in the circle with more stones if needed.

Next, lay a base of tinder made from loose material that should be easy to light and quick to burn. Dry grasses and leaves, small twigs, bark, and even newspaper will all work perfectly. Fill in the circle of rocks with the tinder, forming a base of combustible material.

On top of that, you'll need to lay the kindling. This should be slightly larger material, like thicker twigs and larger leaves, that will accept the fire from the tinder. The material you're using will determine the shape the kindling makes. Long leaves or twigs can be piled up in a pyramid. Looser material, like grass or leaf litter, can be lain down more flatly. Either way, get the material to cover as large an area as possible while leaving enough free space in between for air to reach and to fuel the fire.

On top of the kindling, place your firewood. This should be composed of larger, thicker, slower-burning logs, which will act as the fuel for the fire and keep it burning for as long as possible.

Avoid rotten wood, dense wood, and damp or waterlogged timber. Fill in any larger gaps with more kindling. Light the tinder first and watch it carefully to ensure it does not blow out or spit out a spark that could cause an uncontrollable blaze.

Once it's aflame, do not leave the fire unguarded, and extinguish it fully when you're finished.

11.

HOW TO ESCAPE
A SINKING VEHICLE

Thought being stuck behind the wheel of an out-of-control car was bad enough? How about if the car is careening toward a body of water?

Luckily, as nightmarish a scenario as this may be, by acting coolly and quickly there is a good chance you (and your passengers, should there be any) will be able to escape relatively easily.

As the vehicle heads toward the water, if you're the driver, you should adopt a brace position - holding tightly onto the wheel, with your hands at the standard 10-to-2 position. There's a fair chance the impact will set off the car's airbags, so you'll want to avoid any other position that might result in an inadvertent injury.

A typical car will stay afloat in water anywhere from 30 to 120 seconds, but you should be prepared to act as quickly as possible. The principle here is known as SWO: **S**eatbelts off; **W**indow open (or broken); and **O**ut, children first.

Unbuckle your seatbelt as soon as you hit the water. Just as with oxygen masks on a plane, worry about your seatbelt before helping anyone else with theirs. You won't be able to help anybody if you're still strapped in as well.

Once you're unbuckled, open a window. The water pressure will make opening the door all but impossible, so your window is your only exit. Electric windows should still be operational for a minute or two even after a car has hit the water, so wind down your nearest one - ideally before the water reaches up to it.

If the electrics have failed, you'll need to smash it. Look for anything strong enough to shatter the glass (an ideal tool is the metal prongs that hold in the car's headrests). If there's nothing to hand, maneuver yourself around in your seat and use your legs to kick against the glass with your feet. Front and back windscreens are designed to take impact, so don't try to break those.

With the window gone, get any children out of the vehicle first, then escape yourself. By this point, there may well be a lot of water inside the car so you may have to swim free.

If the window won't budge or break, you'll have to wait. Time may be of the essence, but your last chance is to wait for the pressure inside the car to equalize with that outside, which means waiting until there is sufficient water inside the vehicle. Stay as calm as you can to control your breathing, then take a deep breath as the water reaches chest height. Locate the door handle, and continue trying it as the water pours in. Eventually, the pressure outside and inside will match, and the door should open, allowing you to swim free.

12.

HOW TO MAKE A MAKESHIFT SAILBOAT

You're stranded on an island and, with resources used up, you need to escape. Sounds like someone needs to build a boat!

First up, let's set our sights on the right result here. When we say, "build a boat", we're not going to end up with a five-star ocean liner. We're talking basics: a raft-like hull, ideally with some kind of makeshift sail and shelter. The key points are buoyancy and sturdiness, as you don't want something too heavy to support your weight once you board it, or too flimsy which will drift apart once you set off from the shore.

If you're making a log raft, look for wood that doesn't have too many knots or offshoots, and doesn't feel too heavy, a sign that it may already be waterlogged. Making a raft doesn't necessarily require wood, of course. Barrels, plastic piping, storage containers, and even plastic bottles can be used.

Assemble your raft in shallow water. That way, the water will be able to support the weight of the timbers or parts as you bind them together, and you won't have to exhaust yourself dragging the completed boat down to the waterside.

A single flat sheet of plywood or thin metal makes an ideal base, but if you're not spoilt for material choice, you'll have to assemble a basic frame yourself. Start by linking two planks or timbers with two cross-timbers lain across them to create an open square or rectangle. Bind these four timbers together as tightly as possible where they overlap at the corners. Once this basic frame is assembled, float your remaining logs into place and fasten them to the cross-timbers.

When your final log is in place, keep your raft in shallow water while you test its buoyancy and the strength of your binding. Any gaps in the timbers can be shored up with smaller ones, and any loose knots should be retied or tightened before you begin loading it.

One final point: in a desert island scenario, escaping by raft should be a last resort. The open ocean risks starvation, dehydration, storms, swells, and shipping lanes, all of which could see your Robinson Crusoe adventure come to an abrupt end…

13.

HOW TO CROSS A RIVER

The bridge is down. Or perhaps there is a bridge, but it doesn't look safe. Or perhaps, there wasn't even a bridge there, to begin with. No matter - you just need to get from one side of a river to the other.

First of all, you need to pick a suitable place to cross. Given a choice between rolling, gushing, white-water rapids and a shallow, slow-moving section of a river, the choice should be obvious. Look for a spot where you think you will be able to maintain a straight course from one side to the other and won't be battling against a strong current. An island or sandbank in the middle will help break up longer crossings.

Water tends to move fastest at river bends, so seek out the straightest part that you can find (use a map to do so, if possible) while avoiding S-shaped or C-shaped areas. If you're dealing with an especially meandering river and can only see S-shapes, then your best place to cross will be in the midsection of the S, between its bent sections.

Find out what you're dealing with both depth-wise and current-wise. If you can safely approach the river edge, use a stick or pole to see how deep the water is. If you can't safely get down to the riverside, throw a rock in and listen to the sound it makes. The deeper the water, the louder the *ker-ploosh!*

Ideally, you should only be crossing a river that flows no higher than your knees, but if that's not possible, you should only be wading through water that has little to no current. To find out how fast the water is flowing, toss a stick into the river and see how quickly it is swept away. Even a river that looks sluggish can have a rapid current, so you'll need to be prepared.

The faster the current, the shallower the water you should look for: a good test is to try to walk along the bank faster (or as fast as) the stick as it floats away downstream. If you can't keep up with it, that's a fair sign that the current is too strong for you to match it, and you should seek a different place to cross.

Muddy or murky water can hide underwater obstacles, so check for floating debris on the water's surface or sticks and logs piled against the rocks in the slower parts of the channel. The more you can see there, the more there likely is flowing out of sight below the surface.

When crossing the water, use a stick to help keep at least two points of contact with the riverbed at all times. Keep your eyes up, focusing on the opposite shore. Move your feet slowly and keep them low, feeling out for underwater obstacles. Stick together if there is a group of you, locking arms if the current is strong. Wade at a slight angle, diagonally, against the direction of the current. If the current is too strong, don't press ahead. Turn back and try elsewhere.

14.

HOW TO FIX
A BROKEN BONE

The best treatment for a broken bone? Unsurprisingly, that would be in the emergency room! But if you're stuck somewhere far from help, you'll need a more makeshift solution.

A splint is a strip of rigid material that holds a broken bone in place. If a broken bone isn't immobilized, fractures can drift or fragment further, damaging surrounding tissues.

The shape and size of the splint depend on the bone in question. Fingers and toes can be kept in place by being bound to stiff twigs or even pens and pencils. Hands and feet can be wrapped tightly with fabric bandages easily enough. But broken arms and legs require more careful preparation. The trick is to find something large enough and rigid enough to provide solid support.

In an emergency, thick cardboard, tree branches, bottles, and even rolls of newspaper can all be used in place of ordinary bandages. If the makeshift splint - like a plastic bottle cut down to size - has sharp edges, wrap it in fabric first to protect the skin and keep the wearer comfortable.

Use tape, shoelaces, string, or similar material to fasten the splint around the site of the break but avoid placing them directly over the injury - ideally, the bindings should be tightened just above and just below. The point is to immobilize the limb, but don't fasten the splint too tightly.

Bear in mind the affected bone will need support. A broken arm can easily be placed in a makeshift sling, but a broken leg might require a makeshift stretcher or gurney, with the patient helped to safety and further treatment by other people.

15.

HOW TO KNOW IF
A PLANT IS EDIBLE

Eating even the smallest amount of a toxic plant can cause sickness or even death. Finding food in the wilderness, however, is often imperative, yet how can you find out what plants are and are not edible?

Much of the basics of edibility are obvious. A plant that looks or smells unpleasant, caustic, or rotten, is best avoided. If it passes this first hurdle, try holding the part of the plant you are thinking of eating - whether it is leaves, berries, bark, roots, or tubers - against the inside of your arm or wrist, where the skin is thin and sensitive. Provided there's no adverse reaction, like itchiness or burning, press ahead.

Based on the feel and structure of the plant, decide how you're going to eat it. Woodier plants, roots, and seeds might need cooking or boiling, for example. Even once it's cooked, however, don't dive straight in. Hold another small portion of the prepared plant against your lips and test for any further adverse reaction. So long as you survive that unscathed, try a small amount in your mouth. At this point, anything that still tastes bitter, harsh, or even soapy might well be worth avoiding. Spit it out and wash your mouth out with water. If that first mouthful still causes no adverse reactions, you can assume the plant is safe.

Each stage of this edibility test shouldn't be rushed. Be mindful to give each stage time to react. You don't want to finish a plate of something that felt perfectly fine against your skin, only to feel your lips and wrist start to react while you sit digesting it…

16.

HOW TO BUILD
A ROPE BRIDGE

Every decent bridge needs solid supports or props at either end, from which it can be suspended or attached. Fasten each end of the rope to something immovable, like a boulder or a tree trunk, or else drive wooden stakes into the ground. Whatever secure point you choose, give yourself as much room to maneuver at either end of the bridge as possible. You'll want to get yourself safely on the bridge - and safely across the bridge - far from the edge.

Once the rope is secure, you'll have a single loop spanning the gorge. If you have a second rope or even a climber's carabiner, you can attach yourself to it and hang below, pulling yourself across as if on a manual zipline. If you don't have a way of securing yourself to the rope crossing, you'll have to rely on grip alone - so you'll need to maintain as close a contact with the rope as possible.

Given a looped bridge, the safest way to cross is on all fours. Hold one rope loop in one hand, and the other in the other hand. Rest your feet and legs behind, and then shuffle your way slowly across the bridge, edging your way forward, maintaining four points of contact with the rope loop at all times.

17.

HOW TO MAKE AN AXE

Without a blacksmith to help you out, you'll need to improvise to make a tool like an axe, and your best bet is a stone-headed one.

For that, you'll ideally need four things: a stone blade; a second stone with which to sharpen the blade; a handle; and a rope or cord to fasten it all together.

In picking a suitable blade, you'll want a rock that is already relatively flat, or that flakes when struck and so can be fashioned to a point easily. Flintstones or slate are a good choice, but if you're by the water, river rocks or flagstone-like sea slabs work too, as they're often worn flat by running water and require less beating into shape.

You'll need a handle too, so look for a suitable branch or pole. Younger wood from saplings or fast-growing bushes or shrubs is often a good choice, as it is more flexible and can reshape for use more easily.

To sharpen the blade, strike it against the edge of a larger stone, or knock chips off it using a smaller, handheld stone you can control easily. The blade stone should fragment easily but can still take the weight and power of the chopping you'll need it for. Make sure you pick something that isn't going to shatter into pieces the moment you apply any force to it.

Once sharp, use a rope or cord to tie the blade to the handle. If there's no rope available, try pushing the blade through a thickened, fresher piece of wood so that it passes out the other side. The natural tension of the young wood should be enough to hold the blade in place as you use it.

18.

HOW TO TELL IF
SOMEONE IS LYING

Some people have a sixth sense of when they're being hoodwinked. Other people have a near preternatural ability to disguise when they're talking complete rubbish and lying through their teeth. And somewhere in the middle, you need to know when you're being lied to.

A person who is knowingly lying or misleading you will often find it difficult to maintain their natural speech and conversation patterns. In other words, they're so concerned with convincing you that what they're saying is true that they forget - for want of a better phrase - how to be normal.

Keep your eyes as well as your ears open, because not only will their voice change, but their natural hand gestures may stop matching what they're saying. Think of someone shaking their head in disagreement while coming out with a spoken statement of agreement, and you'll get the idea.

Often, a liar will want to ensure their tracks are well and truly covered and so will "over speak," coming out with many more words than necessary. They might repeat themselves more frequently or start retelling or rephrasing something they have already made clear.

Liars often aren't keen to maintain eye contact, which might result in them not only looking away more frequently but in finding ways to cover or shield their eyes when speaking. That ties in with an excess of nervous, fidgety behavior often exhibited by people when they lie too, so keep an eye out for multiple or unnatural changes of body position, shuffling feet, or for someone who doesn't quite know what to do with their hands. Research has also suggested that liars tend to point more than truth-tellers, especially at other people.

19.

HOW TO SURVIVE EATING SOMETHING YOU SHOULDN'T

Doubtless, you have had food poisoning at some point in your life, so you'll be painfully aware that your body has a perfectly natural way of - er, *ridding itself* of the offending matter as quickly as possible. But what if you've ingested something you really, *really*, shouldn't have?

Just as with food poisoning, the key here is often the same: you need to get that stuff out of you as quickly as possible. Clear anything that is left in your mouth by spitting it out and rinsing your mouth with water.

If you've eaten a poisonous plant, you might want to try inducing vomiting to clear the stomach. As well as placing a finger down the throat, you can always drink a draft of saltwater for much the same effect, or even down a mixture of something foul like mustard and water. Make sure your airway remains clear throughout.

If the quantity you have eaten is not too large, you can try diluting or neutralizing the stomach contents by drinking water or milk. Staying hydrated is equally important with ordinary food poisoning and after allergic reactions too.

These vague rules, however, do not work with all poisons, and nor should they take the place of emergency medical care. If you have ingested something caustic, for instance, vomiting it up can burn to the back of the throat and cause just as much damage as the poison could to your stomach. Likewise, attempting to neutralize or dilute the stomach contents is not always advisable, and so should only be attempted on the advice of medical professionals.

20.

HOW TO SURVIVE A RUN-IN WITH A SWARM OF BEES

So-called Africanized honeybees - or "killer" bees, as they've become known - can be much more reactive and aggressive than ordinary bumblebees or honeybees. So, if you're unlucky enough to encounter a swarm, what's the best way of escaping them?

The most immediate answer is also the most obvious: run. In doing so, however, avoid swatting, batting, or crushing any bees. They're attracted by movement, and this could enrage the swarm and worsen or prolong the encounter.

As you run, pull any loose clothing over any exposed skin. Pull down your shirt sleeves, for instance, and pull your collar up over your head to protect your neck, face, and ears. If that's not possible, cover as much of your face as possible with your hands and arms.

Seek shelter where you can. It might work in the movies, but diving into the water isn't always an ideal escape, as the bees likely won't disperse even while you're below the surface.

The stings are painful but often not serious, though keep a keen eye out for any potential reactions that will require medical attention. You'll also need to remove the stingers from your skin, but don't squeeze them between your fingers or with tweezers, as that can inject more venom into the wound. Instead, scrape them as if scratching an itch, which should dislodge them quickly and safely.

21.

HOW TO SURVIVE
A HEART ATTACK

It's an absolute no-brainer, but the fundamental priority when you or someone else is suffering a heart attack is to call for an ambulance and get swift and immediate emergency care from medical professionals. But what if you're on your own or not easily found or contactable by phone? What can you do to improve your chances of survival?

If you're experiencing any of the classic symptoms of a possible cardiac arrest - intense chest pain, tingling arms, dizziness, breathlessness, cold sweating, and so on - take aspirin to thin your blood and lighten the load on your heart. Rest or lie down if you feel able and take deep steady breaths. Focus on your breathing to try to maintain calm. Do not eat or drink, and certainly do not attempt to drive yourself to an emergency room. If symptoms pass - as they very often do; not everything that feels like a heart attack develops into full cardiac arrest - wait until you feel able to cope, then seek medical help.

22.

HOW TO ESCAPE FROM A LOCKED ROOM

They are a claustrophobic's worst nightmare but escape rooms have been big business in the early 21st century, and their popularity seems to be far from waning. Escaping a locked room that someone has rigged with puzzles is one thing, however. What if you were to find yourself genuinely trapped locked in a room - or, for that matter, locked out of one - and needed to gain entry or escape?

The solution depends on the nature of the lock. So-called privacy doorknobs, in which the locking mechanism is built into the handle itself, can sometimes be picked using something long, thin, and sturdy, like a skewer or a hat pin. Slide your implement of choice into the lock - twisting it around, if necessary - until it catches on the mechanism inside. Applying pressure to the lock should knock the mechanism into place, and the door should click open.

Some locks can be prized open using something more along the lines of a credit card, slid between the door itself and the frame. Pushing the card against the bolt can give you enough purchase to force the lock apart and open the door.

Then again, locks of all kinds can be jimmied open using an improvised lockpick fashioned from anything from a bobby pin to a paperclip. For the best results, however, you ideally need two - one to work as a pick, the other to work as a locksmith's tension wrench (more on which a little later in this book...)

23.

HOW TO TELL IF AN ANIMAL IS VENOMOUS

First of all, a vocabulary lesson. Venom and poison are not the same. A venomous creature has to inject its toxins into flesh or the bloodstream to have an effect. Think a rattlesnake bite. A poisonous creature, on the other hand, has to be actively ingested - eaten, in other words - to have an effect. Think fugu, the toxic Japanese blowfish that can be fatal if incorrectly prepared by a chef.

So, unless you're wandering around the wilderness randomly consuming wild animals (never a good plan), there's more of a chance of you having a run-in with a *venomous* creature than a poisonous one. So, whether you've been bitten by a snake, stung by a scorpion, or trodden on something with an underwater spine while wading in the sea, how do you know if the creature in question is venomous or just dangerously armed?

It's not a particularly comforting thought, but the first hint that something is wrong will come from the site of the puncture wound itself. Venoms are often fast-acting - for good reason, if a snake were to bite a mouse, and the venom was so weak that the mouse could run far away before finally dying, the snake would be left in the unenviable position of having to then track it down.

The faster the venom acts and the faster the prey perishes, the easier it is for the snake to find its meal.

Any intense pain, swelling, seeping, bruising, or flushing of the skin at the site of a bite or sting is a good sign that the creature that inflicted it is indeed packing a venomous punch. More dangerous venoms will start to have whole-body effects within a matter of minutes, too, so keep an eye out for any dizziness, impaired vision, sweating, feverishness, or vomiting. Emergency medical treatment - and if necessary, an antivenom (antivenin) dosage - is a must.

Aside from the effects of the venom itself, many creatures advertise their dangerousness in their coloration. If you're able to get a look at the critter that's caught you, keep an eye out for any bright hues or dazzle patterns. Snakes with thick, triangular-shaped heads are often venomous too, as those thick necks are packed with the muscles needed to bury their fangs deep into their prey's body.

If you're heading out into the wilderness, of course, the best way to identify any potential venomous creature is to educate yourself before you go. Research the local wildlife and familiarize yourself with the kinds of potentially dangerous animals you might come across.

24.

TOP FIVE SURVIVAL HACKS: STICKY TAPE

Far outside of merely wrapping gifts, sticky tape has a multitude of uses. In a survival situation, in fact, tape - and in particular, a roll of thick, heavy-duty tape, like duct tape - might come in far more useful than you might imagine.

1. **START A FIRE IN THE WIND OR RAIN.** Use sticky tape to bind several matches together to make an impromptu firelighter that will hold its flame much more robustly than a single match on its own in windy or rainy conditions. Unlike plastic tapes, duct tape burns away to nothing too, and so will only serve to add fuel to the fire.

2. **FIX YOUR SHOES (AND YOUR FEET).** Not only can tape be used to repair a shoe's aglet (that's the plastic tip of a shoelace, FYI) to stop it from fraying, you can use heavy-duty tape as an improvised bandage to protect your skin and stop uncomfortable shoes from rubbing your heels or toes.

3. **FASHION A CUP.** Duct tape holds its shape so well that its natural waterproof qualities can be harnessed in making cups, pipes, and even small bowls, pails, and plates. Sticking layer upon layer of tape on top of one another will

strengthen it further and allow you to build up the sides of a suitable container.

4. **MAKE A ROPE.** If you've ever tried to tear a roll of sticky tape with your bare hands, you'll know that it is remarkably durable. Harness that durability by scrunching a few layers of tape together - trying to keep the sticky side on the inside—into a long cord that can be used as a makeshift rope.

5. **INSECT REPELLENT.** Okay, so tape alone doesn't have much in the way of a repellent quality, but by taping the bottom of your trousers tight to your legs, or your collars and cuffs to your neck and arms, biting insects can be kept out of anywhere they really shouldn't be.

25.

HOW TO MAKE
A TOURNIQUET

A tourniquet is a tight binding that when correctly applied to a wound - in particular, a bleeding arm or leg - can help stem the flow of lost blood, buying some much-needed time ahead of emergency care. They are not long-term solutions but stopgaps, yet their use can prove lifesaving. So, how can you make one?

Decide first if a tourniquet is necessary by assessing the wound. Blood from a free-flowing wound will not clot without external pressure, so hold a pad of clean absorbent material over the wound - preferably from a first aid kit, but a cotton T-shirt would work just as well in an emergency - and press. Try to disturb the wound as little as possible, as that can prevent natural clotting from taking place. If the wound is too severe, a tourniquet is likely your best option.

Look for something strong and pliable, but not elastic: a leather belt, a necktie, the handle of a handbag, or a fabric bandana would all work well, as would long strips of fabric torn from shirts or jeans. Ideally, it should be a few inches wide; if the tourniquet is too thin, like thread or dental floss, it can snap or loosen (and if applied to somewhere smaller, like a finger, could end up cutting off circulation altogether).

The tourniquet is designed to restrict blood flow, so keep the patient's circulatory system in mind and tie it *between* the heart and the wound. So, if a person had a deep cut on their arm, the tourniquet would go slightly further up the same arm, creating a barrier between blood flow from the heart and the wound.

Bind the tourniquet around two to three inches above the wound if possible; where that isn't possible, as at the knee or elbow joint, you should apply it to the other side of the joint, then keep the joint closed tightly by bending the arm or leg.

Tourniquets should never be used on the head, chest, or trunk. And remember, they're just stopgaps, not permanent solutions, so emergency medical attention is still necessary.

26.

HOW TO SURVIVE
A SNAKE ATTACK

If you've been bitten by a venomous snake, remain as still and as calm as possible. The main aim is to slow the spread of the venom throughout your body system, so increasing your heart rate and blood flow by running or panicking is not going to help.

Keep the site of the wound below the level of your heart - so do not hold the affected body part above your head, for instance. Remove any tight clothing or jewelry from the affected area, as these can cause even more trauma if it starts to swell.

Keep the wound clean, with soap and water, if possible, but do not scrub it vigorously as this won't help to "wash" the venom out and could instead push it deeper into your flesh. Bandage the wound and seek immediate medical treatment.

Not all snakes are venomous, of course. Say you're trekking through the Amazon and suddenly find yourself up against a monstrously powerful anaconda, intent on constricting the life out of you. Constricting snakes can grow to more than 30ft and weigh upward of 500lbs (and take down prey more than their body weight with ease). If one leaps out at you, you're going to have a fight on your hands.

The snake will instinctively try to wrap its coils around you. Whenever you exhale and your chest drops in size, the snake will tighten its coils to prevent you from inhaling as much of the next breath you take. Holding your breath will buy you some much-needed time.

Enormous snakes are nothing but muscle and teeth, but they have their vulnerabilities. If you have a free hand or foot, go on the offensive. Stamping, tugging, or even biting at the snake's sensitive tail will cause it intense pain, as will aiming blows at its eyes, nostrils, or snout.

If the snake has bitten you, remember its teeth are not venomous, but they are designed not to let go. An anaconda's fangs are backwards-facing, so instinctively pulling yourself free - against the direction of its teeth - could cause more injury than the bite itself. Instead, push yourself slightly further into its throat to free yourself from its teeth, which may well instinctively cause the snake to slacken its grip. Then, if you're able, haul yourself free.

27.

HOW TO MAKE
A LIFE PRESERVER

The key to a life preserver is its buoyancy, which is provided by air either forced into or naturally a part of whatever material you use. Wood has natural air pockets that make it float in water, and so any wooden debris floating on the surface of the water can be used to help you to stay afloat when required. In true survival scenarios, however, even your clothes can be used to fashion a makeshift life jacket.

It's a technique used and practiced by the military all over the world: blowing or "scooping" air into water-saturated clothing, like shirt sleeves or even trousers, makes an impromptu float. The water in the fibers of the cloth prevents the air on the inside from escaping as quickly as it would normally and tying off the openings keeps the air in place. It's even possible to achieve a similar effect by blowing into the open neckline of a shirt to "inflate" it, then tugging against it so that it forms a water-based seal around your neck to keep the air in place.

28.

HOW TO WALK
WITHOUT BEING HEARD

Slowing your pace, watching out for potential noise-making obstacles, and placing your feet carefully on the ground will of course remove the sound from walking. But what else can you do?

Keeping slightly crouched will help you to control your steps more acutely. Rather than letting all your weight come down noisily at once, a crouched position will be easier to silence as it will engage more of your leg muscles as you walk, so that you can control your weight more deliberately.

Walk toe to heel, keeping your weight on the back of your back foot, and placing your front foot softly on the ground, toes first. When walking upstairs, hold yourself close against the wall, so that you're applying pressure not to the middle of the stair but to the edge of the tread where it's far less likely to creak.

29.

HOW TO SURVIVE
A PLANE CRASH

How much of the air steward's pre-flight emergency demonstrations do you *actually* take in? These days, flying is such a commonplace activity for many people that it's all too tempting to keep your head down and your headphones in. Should the unimaginable happen, however, that pre-flight demonstration may well save your life - as could some of these other hints and tips air crash survivors have found helpful over a century of travel.

Familiarize yourself with your position in the plane, so that if the cabin were to fill with smoke or the lights were to fail on a red-eye, you could count the rows of seats in front or behind you to find your way out in the dark.

Statistically, you have a better chance of survival at the rear of the craft, too - and though we all love a window seat, sitting on an aisle at the rear of the plane will ensure you escape the craft quickly. Keep your seatbelt tight and fastened at all times, even while you sleep, in case of an emergency while you're snoozing.

If the plane starts going down, adopt the brace position recommended by the air steward: if the seat in front is close enough, they may tell you to brace yourself against that, or else bend over and hold your head between your knees. In both instances, keep your seat upright, and your feet flat on the floor.

After an emergency landing, there may well be a fire producing clouds of thick, noxious smoke. Use clothing (preferably moistened, if you have a bottled drink at hand) to cover your mouth and nose. Keep low to the floor where the air is clearer. Leave the plane from your closest exit - leaving everything behind, no matter how valuable - and get at least 160 yards from the wreckage in case of an explosion.

If the plane lands on water, put on your life jacket, but do not inflate it until you're outside. If the plane is burning, swim away from the wreckage but avoid, drifting or splitting from other passengers.

All this being said, air travel remains the safest form of travel, with the odds of anything untoward happening in the air becoming vanishingly unlikely with every passing year. Even if something does happen, however, more than 90% of air crashes have survivors, so knowing some basic survival tips may well prove invaluable.

30.

HOW TO SURVIVE
A METEOR STRIKE

Let's be honest, if there's an apocalyptically gigantic block of space rock hurtling toward Earth, chances are no amount of survival hacks will help the explosive vaporization that its impact will create. That being said, you can at least make a few changes before the event to increase your chances of survival and - should you wish to - make preparations to survive after the impact too.

With 70% of Earth being covered in water, it's more likely an asteroid will strike the sea than the land, which makes tsunami-like impact waves a potentially devastating problem. Head inland and uphill to offset the danger.

Earth's surface is likely going to become unlivable, so a bunker is your best bet. Pack it with enough food and water to survive several months and look for sources of renewable energy. Batteries, torches, and lightbulbs will be paramount too, as well as fuel, medical supplies, communications devices, and a radio to maintain contact with the outside world.

Supplies will likely need to be rationed, as there's no telling how long the aftereffects of an impact will last. For the same reason, best take something underground to keep your mind engaged - be it books, music, musical instruments, games, sports equipment, or whatever hobby you now have a fair few months to pursue.

31.

HOW TO PERFORM
A TRACHEOTOMY

Choking is a medical emergency and performing a tracheotomy - cutting a hole in a person's airway so that they can breathe - is itself an emergency procedure that should only be undertaken as a last resort.

If you suspect someone is choking, alert the emergency services and prepare to administer the Heimlich maneuver. From behind, wrap your arms around their body, just below their ribcage, with your fist pressed lightly into the center of their trunk below the breastbone. Jolt them upward so that your fist presses up into their chest. The force of each jolt will force air out of their lungs, to dislodge whatever is stuck in their airways with a burst of air. Repeat if necessary.

Only if a person is no longer able to breathe on their own and loses consciousness should a tracheotomy ever be attempted. Using a sharp knife, make an incision just below the Adam's apple (you may need to feel for this with your fingers) and just above the cricoid cartilage - a ridge of bony cartilage at the top of the windpipe.

Make a half-inch cut, roughly a half-inch deep - sufficient to part the skin and open the airways, so that the wound acts as a breathing hole. Keep the wound open with a rigid tube, like a drinking straw or the plastic cylinder of a pen. CPR can be administered by breathing down the tube rather than into the patient's mouth, alternating breaths with chest compressions until emergency medical care is available.

32.

HOW TO SURVIVE FALLING THROUGH ICE

Few things could be as nightmarish as falling through an ice-covered river or lake - especially if you find yourself swept under the ice by currents and trapped in freezing water. No matter the situation, it only takes around ten minutes for hypothermia to set in, so time is limited. It all sounds like an impossible situation to escape. So, what can you do?

If you fall through the ice and remain afloat where you've fallen through, stay calm. Flailing your arms wastes valuable body heat, and panicked breathing in such cold temperatures may cause you to hyperventilate. Your instinct will be to haul yourself back out onto the ice with your hands - as if getting out the side of a swimming pool - but applying your body weight to such a small part of the edge of the ice will likely just cause it to buckle and collapse. Instead, try to float horizontally and slide your entire body back up onto the ice, covering as much of the edge as possible to spread your weight around. Once out, don't try to stand, as that risks you falling back in or the ice breaking once again. Instead, slide your way back to shore.

If you find yourself trapped under the ice, your immediate priority is not to get out, but to get air. If you're unable to get back to the hole you fell through, you must find another breathing hole or a point where the ice is weaker so you can force your way through to oxygen. Remember, ice is never the same thickness everywhere across a body of water. Lakes tend to freeze from the edges inward, so thinner ice may well be found further away from the shore. The ice closer to the shoreline, conversely, may be frozen solid right down to the bed.

If the ice is thin enough to break through from below, you may find you have more strength kicking with your legs than pushing with your hands. Once you've made a hole, take a few deep breaths to help control your breathing and then try to escape as before.

33.

HOW TO OPEN
A STUCK JAR

If the lid of a jar is metal, heating it in hot water (or even will a hairdryer or cigarette lighter) will cause the metal to expand and likely pop the seal, allowing you to open it. You might also be able to pop it by simply tapping or knocking around the edge of the metal lid with a heavy spoon or rolling pin, or by prying something narrow - like a metal spatula or a butter knife - under the edge of the lid so that air can enter the jar and pop the seal that way.

Another way is to tilt the jar to a 45° angle and slap the base of it with your other hand. The impact will push the contents of the jar downward toward the lid, increasing the pressure of the air beneath it, which should be enough to pop the seal from inside and loosen the cap.

Alternatively, you can open a jar by using something to give you a better purchase on the lid than your hand alone can manage. A household rubber glove or a dry dishtowel might suffice, or else you can try wrapping the lid in plastic kitchen wrap, a dryer sheet, or even a thick rubber band to get a better grip that way.

34.

HOW TO SURVIVE A CROCODILE ATTACK

Survive. Crocodile attack. Those words don't seem to fit together really, do they?

After all, crocodiles are some of nature's deadliest creatures, and their ambush-and-grab hunting technique seems to leave little chance of escape. In fact, your best chance of surviving a crocodile attack is to avoid its jaws in the first place: once a crocodile's mouth latches onto something - with a force of 3,700 pounds per square inch (compared to around 100 for a human being) - it will do everything in its power not to open them again. And heck, that's a lot of power.

If they're not intent on making you their next meal, a crocodile might bite down on you and immediately release you, as a warning blow. If that's the case, get yourself away from the animal as quickly as possible. If you're unlucky enough to have the croc bite down and hold on, of course, your need to act accordingly.

Nine out of ten croc attacks occur on or near water, as crocodiles deal with their prey by dragging it below the surface. (Chances are you'll drown before you're eaten as if that was any consolation.) If the croc indeed attacks you in the water, you'll need to right yourself and keep your head above the water's surface as long as possible.

Your best bet now is to fight back. With teeth, claws, thick scales, and an immensely strong thrashing tail, crocodiles might seem invulnerable, but their eyes are a weak spot. Gouge, kick, or punch them as hard as you can, and do not stop until you are free. Any bystanders can assist by battering the croc's head with sticks, logs, rocks, or even oars.

If your hand is in the croc's mouth, aim for the palatal valve - an epiglottis-like flap at the back of the throat that prevents water from getting into the animal's lungs. Tugging or punching that, will cause water to flood the creature's throat.

On land, your best bet with a croc encounter is to run. Crocodiles are fast, but over short distances, humans are faster. (Just remember to run *away* from water, as if there is one crocodile in the vicinity, chances are there are more elsewhere.)

35.

HOW TO LIVE IN ANTARCTICA

Antarctica is the coldest, driest, highest, and windiest continent. It's so inhospitable that it's also technically the world's largest desert. Parts of it are covered in ice 1.24 miles thick, on average (though in some places that reaches more than twice as much). It has few plants, and relatively few animals, is in permanent darkness for half the year, and it has the greatest concentration of volcanoes of any other continent on the planet. All told, it's a fairly difficult place to call home.

Should you want to, of course, how could you live there? Well, these days, there are several permanent research stations there, fitted with such mod cons as a barber's shop and an ATM. Outside of those facilities, however, air temperatures can fall to below –94°F, winds can blow at 200mph, blizzards can deposit several feet of snow in a matter of minutes, and there is perpetual darkness for six months of the year. Surviving on your own is a different matter.

Finding shelter would be the immediate concern. Though Antarctica is covered in wide and endless snow plains, there are mountains and escarpments, the leeward sides of which would at least provide some shelter. You could scarcely survive the temperatures without specialist clothing and equipment, however, and there is no firewood to gather.

Food would be another problem. At the coast and the surrounding islands, there are dense fisheries and enormous amounts of shellfish. In the barren continental interior, you'd have little to go on besides penguin meat (which is fatty and oily, and that's without a fire to cook it on).

So, survival here is possible but depends on what part of the continent you're attempting to survive in, and what resources you have with you when you're there. Without food or shelter, however, Earth's most inhospitable continent offers little chance of any prolonged existence.

36.

HOW TO ESCAPE
A BURNING BUILDING

The American Red Cross suggests that, on average, you only have somewhere in the region of two minutes to escape a burning building before the effects of heat and smoke prove too much.

With the correct equipment, small domestic fires can be dealt with, but never attempt to extinguish larger fires yourself. Your priority is to escape. If possible, close doors and windows behind you to slow the spread of the fire. If your normal escape route is blocked by fire or smoke, find another way out. That route may be a window; if you're upstairs, throw quilts, blankets, pillows, cushions, and even clothing out of the window to cushion your landing if you're forced to jump.

If you suspect a fire is raging on the other side of a door, feel the temperature of the door and the door handle with your hand, to assess how bad or how near the fire may be.

If your escape route is filled with smoke, keep low to the ground where the air is clearer. Use clothing to cover your mouth and nose while using your hands to feel for obstacles. If your clothing catches fire, extinguish it immediately - stop, drop, and roll - to minimize burns and injuries that may otherwise slow your escape.

If your way out is blocked, you may need to await rescue. Retreat to as safe a room as possible. Close any doors and block any gaps or air vents around them, ideally with wet towels. Smoke inhalation is your main danger, not the fire itself, and so stopping it from getting into your refuge is your main concern.

37.

HOW TO GUT AND CLEAN A FISH

If your fish isn't already dead from being out of the water, you'll need to stun it with a stout blow to the head to render it unconscious, and then either "spike" its brain with an incision behind the eye (the most humane way of killing it) or use a blade to remove the head. However, gutting and fileting the fish will be easier with the head still attached.

Rinse the fish clean and remove its tough fins and tail. Holding its body at a 45° angle, use the dull edge of the blade to scrape off its scales in long downward movements, moving against the grain of the scales themselves. Flip the fish over and repeat this on the other side. Once completed, rinse away any loose scales.

Slide the tip of the knife into the fish's underbelly, just inside the tail end. Keeping a firm grip on the knife, cut downward toward the head, and open the body up to remove the guts. If the head is still attached, reach in just behind it and pinch, disconnecting the internal organs where they connect to the head, and pulling them out. Do the same at the tail end, under the inside is clean. Rinse out the cavity with more water and remove the head if required.

38.

HOW TO DEAL WITH
A PANIC ATTACK

Panic attacks can be terrifying, embarrassing, and demoralizing. Knowing how to deal with one, ultimately, is a worthwhile bit of psychological know-how.

As soon as you feel a panic attack building, begin to control your breathing. Take a long, slow breath in, hold it, and then breathe out slowly, for as long - if not longer - than you were breathing in. Continue breathing like this, focusing on the slow and controlled movement of your chest.

Focus your thoughts and concentrate on your surroundings to ground yourself. Try to name five things you can see; four things you can feel; three things you can hear; two things you can smell; and something you could taste. Quiz yourself with simple games, naming an A to Z of countries, cities, movies, sports, or pop groups, for instance.

Realize what it is that is happening to you and how what you are feeling is the natural consequence of a bodily glitch. Your body has, wrongly, released the same swirling cocktail of signals that you would need to escape from a charging lion. The reason you are feeling panicked is that those response chemicals are still in your system, and you will continue to feel panicked until they have worn off. As your system begins to calm down and the chemical signals dissipate, concentrate on your calmness, and focus on regathering your thoughts.

39.

HOW TO MAKE
A BOW AND ARROW

To make a simple bow, you'll need a piece of wood that is dry, but not brittle, and flexible, but not fresh. Fresh green wood is often too pliant to fire an arrow sufficiently well, while older wood will snap rather than bend naturally.

Find the wood's natural curvature by holding one end against your foot and the other in your hand and using your free hand to push outward, away from you, at its middle. The wood will turn along its natural curve; the side facing inward, toward you, is known as its belly. Shape the bow by carving or shaving any knotted or inflexible points in its timber on the belly side only. Your aim is for the bow to make a perfectly smooth curve when you apply pressure in the middle of it so that the arrow will fire as straight as possible.

Make notches at either end through which to pass the bowstring. A suitable string should not in itself be flexible or elastic; the projecting power in a bow comes from the bent wood, not the cord. With the string in place, loop the bow around a branch and pull downward on the string - a process called tillering - so check that it stretches sufficiently, and the bow bends evenly. Make adjustments and continue carving its shape where necessary, until the bow makes a perfectly smooth shape when tillered.

Arrows can simply be made from straight sticks sharpened or whittled to a point. Bent wood can be straightened using heat from the embers of a fire, which can also be used to scorch and blacken the arrow tip to harden it. Make a small notch (called a nock) in the unsharpened end to accommodate the bowstring, and you'll be ready to shoot.

40.

HOW TO FIND WATER
IN THE DESERT

There are entire underground reservoirs, aquifers, and streams below the Sahara Desert. Knowing that isn't very useful when you're stranded on the surface with no water and in 45°C heat, of course, so where can you find water in the desert?

Depending on the desert, there may well be a plentiful supply of cacti. These botanical behemoths hoard water like gold, and it's a popular legend that hacking into a cactus is the desert equivalent of opening a bottle of Evian.

Unfortunately, most cacti aren't keen to give up their water quite so freely, and many of them mix their life-giving H_2O with various toxins that are unpalatable at best and downright dangerous at worst. There are a few exceptions (the prickly pear's fruits can be eaten raw), but cacti as a rule aren't quite as immediately helpful as they might seem. A better bet, so long as you have the equipment, is to make a solar still.

Dig a shallow hole and place a vessel of some sort at the bottom. Over the top, place some kind of impermeable sheeting, like polythene plastic, and weigh the center down with a stone or more sand, so that it forms a funnel shape pointing down into the cup below.

As the air beneath the sill heats up, moisture in the surrounding earth and sand will be drawn out and will condense against the inside of the sheeting, and trickle down the funnel into the cup.

41.

HOW TO HOTWIRE
A CAR ENGINE

Most newer cars have adopted security features that make "hotwiring" the engine to start it, a thing of the past. However, if you have an earlier (think mid-1990s or before) model vehicle - and are in a survival situation that means you really need to get on the road - hotwiring may still be an option.

Remove the plastic covering on the steering column to expose the car's wiring connectors. There will likely be three sets: two will connect to the operators on either side of the steering column, like the indicator lights, while the other will connect to the car's ignition system.

The ignition bundle will contain a wire for the battery (often red); a wire for the starter (often yellow), and a wire for the ignition (often brown or blue). Wrench these wires out, and, if necessary, strip some of the insulting covering from their ends.

Touching the exposed metal of the battery and ignition wires together will start the car's electrics. If you need to start the car itself, however, you'll need to touch the battery wire to the starter wire. This can be extremely dangerous, but with the ignition on, the two exposed wires together should be enough to start the engine and allow you to drive away.

42.

HOW TO STITCH
A WOUND

If you have a wound bad enough to require stitching, then hopefully you're also in a position to have it done by a medical professional. If not, you're in for a difficult and painful time - though not an impossible one.

Many first aid kits now contain portable suturing kits, which will contain a sterilized medical-grade needle, thread, scissors, and a so-called needle driver - a pincer-like tool that holds the needle.

Use the driver to pick up the threaded needle, which will likely be slightly U-shaped. Beginning around half an inch from the side of the wound, make an incision with the needle at a 90° angle. Do not go too deep.

Twist the driver so that the needle passes across the wound and pokes back up through the skin on the other side, around the same distance from where you went in. Pull the thread through the wound, drawing it closed, and leaving around two inches of thread to play with. Tie an overhand knot across the wound by passing the tip of the driver through a loop of thread. Trim off the excess.

Make your sutures individually, producing a run of separate knots known as interrupted stitching. It might be tempting to connect them all with a single thread as if fixing a hole in a garment, but individual stitches are the safest and easiest option for non-professionals in emergencies.

43.

HOW TO SURVIVE
A NIGHT IN THE DESERT

Deserts are the hottest places on Earth and surviving there at all requires finding food and clean water in one of the most inhospitable habitats. At night, however, temperatures can plummet; even in the Sahara, night-time temperatures can fall away to 24.8°F. So how can you survive there?

With temperatures as extreme as that, your priority at night is staying warm. If you're able to start a fire, with whatever wood or debris you have at hand, doing so will immediately improve your chances of survival.

You may have removed layers of clothing to stay cool during the daytime, which you will be better off putting back on after dark. Remember, multiple layers of clothing trap warm air between them, providing better insulation than single layers.

Natural shelters, like caves or overhangs, will be more likely to trap warmed air than the open desert, so nighttime is a good time to try to find a more permanent base. Depending on where in the world you are, of course, some less than hospitable creatures may have got there first, so approach desert caves carefully.

If you need to find help, however, the cooler temperatures of the evening and the morning are good times to travel on foot.

Walking the desert during the day risks suffering from heat exhaustion or sunstroke, so find the right balance between staying put and staying warm and searching for rescue.

44.

HOW TO SURVIVE
A FLASH FLOOD

If you're caught outdoors in the middle of a deluge, how can you ensure you'll escape the flood in one piece?

Whether in a car or on foot, the basic advice is always the same: turn back, and head to shelter or high ground immediately. Make no attempt to cross, drive, or wade through flood waters as they can be deceptively deep, fast-flowing, and full of debris.

If you're unable to head back, however, you may well need to press on to reach safety, in which case move slowly but purposefully, ensuring as strong a foothold as possible before moving forward. Holding a stick or pole will give an extra point of contact if necessary. Plus, it can be used to feel for underwater debris and blown drain covers, and to knock floating debris out of the way.

If the worst happens and you're swept away, try to right yourself in the water and float on your back, feet first to cushion any blows against buildings or obstacles. Never try to drift or swim under floating debris, as there may be more tangled beneath the surface, which you may then become tangled in. If you're able to, aim for areas of stiller, shallower water and make your way to safety.

45.

HOW NOT TO BE YOUR OWN WORST ENEMY

In a book that deals with the dangers of the world, it's easy to forget that your own negative thoughts can be just as destructive as a tornado or a crocodile. So, how can you keep those dark thoughts at bay, and not be your own worst enemy?

One particularly toxic trait is to hold onto thoughts and memories of things that happened in the past. We all tend to look back and cringe at our most embarrassing or humiliating escapades, but if the memories of the past are ruining your future, you need to let them go. Realize that the past has happened and is unchangeable. What is *ahead* can always be changed and is still fully within your control.

Get to know yourself as best as possible. Know your likes and dislikes, abilities and capabilities, and limits and limitations. Doing so might require quiet introspection, but the better you know yourself, the less likely you will be to err in the future by setting targets and aims you have no real chance of achieving and priming yourself for failure before you've even begun.

Realize that time off is as important as time on. Constantly working or toiling is a one-way path to exhaustion and demoralization, so be kind to yourself. Give yourself headspace and downtime. Prioritize yourself.

46.

HOW TO SEW

It's easy to think of sewing as little more than cross-stitches of seascapes. In a survival situation, however, knowing how to sew could help you do everything from repairing torn shoes to keeping the rain out of an overnight shelter.

A key to ensuring a good stitch is to tightly and securely tie off your sewing at both the beginning and the end. Make a slipknot to secure your thread when you start sewing and tie off your thread at the end by forming a loop and passing your needle and thread through them to fasten it in place.

Remember there is more than one type of stitch. A simple running stitch, with each subsequent passing through of the needle and thread arranged in a row, is the simplest stitch ideal in most situations. A back stitch, which uses a one-step-forward-and-two-steps-back pattern, can be used to reinforce a running stitch, by resewing individual stitches.

Zigzagging stitches can be used to link frayed edges or join separate pieces of fabric. And a so-called whip stitch, in which a series of individual stitches are made around the edge of a piece of fabric, can be used to bind the edges of a piece of cloth to stop it from fraying.

47.

HOW TO FIND FRESH WATER

Finding fresh water can be the difference between life or death in certain survival situations, so being able to spot the kinds of signs that might hint at a nearby water supply is important. Obviously, you want to be on the lookout for fresh green vegetation, especially in otherwise dry arid environments like mountainsides or deserts. From a high point, like a hilltop or outcrop, look for obvious tree lines or scattered groups of plants or trees in the landscape too. They might be surrounding a small lake or even lining the course of a stream or creek.

It's not just you that needs the water, of course, so follow animal tracks and bird calls. The denser the tracks, the more animals will have passed by, which may well hint at a useful water source. Look for circling flocks of birds, which may well be surrounding a pool or watering hole. They're an annoyance at the best times, but biting insects and flies, like mosquitos, need water in which to lay their eggs, so even their presence in an area can be a useful sign.

Not all water will be immediately accessible. Remember snow and ice are just freshwaters trapped in their solid form. In deserts and arid locations, look for darker patches of earth or soil on the cooler, shadier sides of dunes or outcrops. Even though it may not be on the surface, water will naturally pool in lower regions and so the water table may still be accessible just below the surface.

48.

HOW TO PRESERVE FOOD

In a survival scenario, maintaining a supply of food will obviously be crucial. But stopping what food you have from spoiling will prove just as important.

Nowadays, there are technological solutions to long-term food storage issues - like vacuum sealing machines and food dehydrators - which any self-respecting doomsday prepper will no doubt be aware of. By removing all the air from food and packing it in airtight plastic, such machines will not only ensure your food will not spoil but can reduce the amount of space needed to store it too.

All the traditional methods of long-term storage are still perfectly valid, of course, so do not overlook the likes of pickling, salting, and curing as means of prolonging the shelf life of your larder. Such techniques have withstood the test of time for so long throughout our history because they are so successful and can help to keep even fresh produce, like fruits and vegetables, edible for many months at a time.

49.

HOW TO SURVIVE
IN A CAVE

In a survival situation, a cave might seem like a ready-made shelter. Protected from the wind and rain, it effectively puts a natural roof over your head. But to make your newfound house a home, you may still need some hints and tips.

Out in the wilderness, anything from bears and pumas to hibernating snakes may have thought the same as you and made the cave their home, so always approach its entrance with caution. Even if there is no animal inside when you get there, look for signs of recent use: blood, bones, and strong-smelling droppings are a surefire sign to keep away.

The geography of some caves means that they trap air that has been warmed during the day, and so will remain warm even after dark. That's helpful in climates where the temperature falls after dark but means caves can become stifling during the hottest parts of the day, so be prepared to vacate if necessary. You'll want to think about ventilation too when it comes to lighting fires to stay warm or cook food.

If your cave shelter is little more than a rocky depression, then you should be able to find decent shelter toward the back. If your cave continues below ground, however, don't be tempted to explore. As well as the threat of becoming trapped below ground, caves can flood rapidly, so it's always best to keep your explorations on the surface until help arrives.

50.

HOW TO WIN
A FIST FIGHT

It's fair to say most of us would never actively choose to be in a fight, but sometimes situations like this, choose us. So, if you even find yourself having to quite literally fight your corner, how best can you do it?

A major part of staying strong in a fight is not the strength of your blows, but the strength of your stance. Stand upright as solidly as you can, with your feet apart and your non-dominant foot in front. (Not sure what that is? It's the foot you *wouldn't* naturally go to kick a ball with.) Keep your weight on your dominant back foot and your knees slightly bent. Angle yourself away from your opponent to control the distance between you more effectively.

Yes, you're going to fight, but you also need to protect yourself, so keep your mouth closed, your chin down, and raise your hands to cover your face and neck when not landing blows.

When punching, imagine you're aiming with your first two fingers - index and middle - and target your blows at natural weak or sensitive spots like the nose or chin. Keep light on your feet and move quickly and agilely (a moving target is harder to aim at, after all). If your opponent successfully dodges a blow, remember they may have had to take a step back or shift their stance or weight to do so, taking them momentarily off balance or taking them briefly off their guard. Be quick to act and capitalize on any such momentary lapse.

51.

HOW TO CLIMB
A TREE

Assess the quality of the tree's timber, and steer clear of anything that looks dry or brittle, as it may not support your weight - especially among the thinner branches furthest from the ground. Be mindful of the recent weather too, as even on a hot day, trees can still be wet from recent rainfall, and your shoes may well be muddy or slippery.

Look for solid foot and handholds, which will be naturally formed by the angles where branches and boughs meet one another. A foot jammed into a natural joint in the tree's foliage will be much more secure than one balanced on the middle of a round branch.

When you start your climb if you can reach the lowest branch, use it to haul yourself up and begin your ascent. If you cannot, you'll either have to jump to reach it or work your way up the trunk, gripping its body as if hugging it with your arms and legs. Remember, branches are always strongest nearer to the ground, and nearer to the trunk itself, so stay as close to the central stalk of the tree as possible.

From the first branch upward, the foliage will likely become denser, so finding your next handhold or foothold should become easier. As you continue upward, however, move only one arm or leg into place at a time, maintaining three points of contact with the tree at all times. The branches will become thinner and greener toward the top of the tree, so know your limits and stop climbing when it looks as if the timber will no longer support your weight.

52.

HOW TO TREAT
AN ANIMAL BITE

If an animal bite is relatively minor, you may well be able to treat it at home by keeping it clean, using ointment to soothe and sterilize the skin, and applying a bandage to protect it as it heals. If the wound is more major, however, emergency treatment will be necessary - and if that's not an immediate option, you'll have to be prepared to treat it yourself.

If the wound is bleeding, cover it and apply pressure. Ideally, you should use a soft towel or gauze from a sterile first aid kit to press down on the wound, but without those at hand, any available fabric will do. Broken bones or particularly deep wounds will have to be dealt with accordingly (more on this in other chapters of this book).

If you can't get to a medical professional, you'll have to clean and bandage the wound with what you have available. Even if the bleeding stops and the wound can be covered, however, an infection is still a real concern. Be mindful of any itching at the site of the bite, as well as feverishness, shivering, vomiting, or dizziness that may be a sign of an infection that would require antibiotic medication. Seek medical attention as soon as you can.

53.

HOW TO MAKE
A SLINGSHOT

The basis of a slingshot is, of course, a sturdy Y-shaped frame, ideally built or shaped from solid, unbending wood. Remember this needs to be portable and handheld, so look for a piece that fits easily in one hand and will not shatter or bend when the sling is pulled back. Wood that is too young or too wet can be strengthened using heat from a fire but be careful not to burn or scorch the wood as this can have the opposite effect.

Use a sharp knife to carve a small nock or notch close to the top of each prong in which to sit the sling securely. Around an inch, or so from the top of the prong should be a position that will give enough stretch and purchase in the sling, without risking the prongs snapping.

Any elastic or similarly stretchy material can be used to make the sling. The shorter you cut it, the more power you will be able to fire the shot with, but the harder the sling itself will be to pull back.

Experiment with different materials and lengths until you have the ideal sling. Fasten either both ends of one long, broad strip to the prongs to create a single-line sling or cut two identical lengths of material and fasten one end of one piece to one prong and the other to the other prong. You can then create a makeshift pouch from a small square of fabric and fasten that in the middle to hurl larger objects.

54.

HOW TO BUILD
A MAKESHIFT CANOE

If you find yourself lost in the middle of nowhere, escaping back to civilization may well involve locating a water source and navigating it back to the nearest town. And among the simplest watercraft to construct is a single-person canoe.

For a truly authentic experience, of course, you'll want to carve your canoe from the timber of a single felled tree. If time and materials are not on your side, of course, you might need to improvise: a perfectly usable vessel can be built from a sheet of plastic or tarpaulin, stretched around a basic frame of interlocking twigs, reeds, or softwood.

Look for bendable green wood, not damp or brittle old wood, and if necessary, use strong grasses or reeds in place of string or cord to bind them together and into shape. Your frame will need a keel, plus several long horizontal poles running the full length of the canoe (the length of which will depend on your height and frame).

To make the frame, imagine you're making an enormous letter H: the poles running the length of the canoe are the uprights, and the horizontal line is a rib connecting them together. In practice, you'll need to bind the vertical struts at the top and bottom of the canoe, along with the keel to form the bottom. You'll also need many more of those crosswise rib sections, bound into the place like a series of U-shaped running the full length of the vessel.

Once you have the basic body constructed, use the plastic sheeting to line the inside and form a waterproof surface on which to sit.

55.

HOW TO START
A FIRE WITH A BATTERY

Depending on the type of battery at your disposal, there are several ways you can start a fire with a battery.

Smashing the glass of a lightbulb and holding its screwed end to a battery terminal will allow you to use its incandescent filament to spark a fire, for instance, and even steel wool can be ignited in much the same way. With just the basics at hand, however, you can use a battery to light a fire using nothing more than a small piece of foil - the kind you may well find wrapped around a piece of chewing gum, a homemade sandwich, or a carton of yoghurt or fruit juice.

Take a very narrow strip of flattened foil, only a few inches in length. Trim down or squash the center of the strip to form a thin filament; it is this that will create the flame.

Hold one end of the strip to one battery terminal, and lightly touch the other end to the other terminal. Work quickly - the spark will be instantaneous, so be sure to hold the burnable filament against your kindling so that you do not lose the spark.

56.

HOW TO TREAT
A BURN

When you have a first aid kit at hand, treating a burn is unpleasant but perfectly simple. Keep the wound cool and sterile, wrap it in bandages, and seek medical attention if necessary. Out in the wilderness, however, dealing with a burn without the usual supplies can be difficult, yet the main first aid principles remain the same.

If the burn is not too severe, use cold, wet compresses to cool the skin. If the skin isn't broken, any water will do as the risk of infecting the wound is limited; if the skin is open or blistered, only clean water should be used.

The skin in and around a burn will be tender, prone to infection, and easily damaged, so bandage it carefully. A dry, non-stick dressing from a first aid kit is ideal, but if you must use a makeshift replacement, try to keep the wound as clean as possible. If the wound is oozing, moisten the bandage with water to avoid damaging the skin more when you remove it.

57.

HOW TO FIX
A PUNCTURE

No doubt all of us will have popped a wheel at some point in our lives, but there is a considerable difference between repairing a bicycle tire with a puncture repair kit and fixing a blowout in the middle of nowhere with limited equipment. So, if you're in the latter group, not the former, how can you mend a puncture in a survival scenario?

If a tire has torn or burst beyond repair, your options are understandably limited. Damage limited only to the tread area, however, is usually manageable and repairable, though may limit the speed and endurance of your vehicle until a new tire can be sourced.

Most puncture repair kits work by placing or injecting a sticky, epoxy rubber material into or over the hole, forming a sufficient sear to maintain the tire. Kits that contain sealant equipment like these can be bought at most garages and are a useful addition to any in-vehicle emergency bag. Use the directions on the kit to use it appropriately; you may need to remove the wheel first in order to apply the rubberized patches some kits contain, so always keep a jack and wrench at hand even if you don't have a spare wheel too.

58.

HOW TO OPEN HANDCUFFS

Most handcuffs use a fairly standard locking mechanism, so undoing them in the same way as picking a lock should open them easily. If you're the one wearing the handcuffs, however, understandably that task becomes a little trickier. But so long as you have some basic supplies, you should still be able to free yourself.

The key (quite literally) is to use a paperclip or bobby pin to make a makeshift lockpick. With your hands restrained, you'll need to use your teeth to unfold the clip into a flat piece of metal, then fold it at one end to make an L-shape.

Place the shorter end of the L into the lock and bend it backwards along your wrist. Remove it, and you should now have two right-angled bends in the metal, forming a rough Z-shape.

Insert this crooked tip into the lock again, and wiggle it around, using the longer tip to gain purchase. You're aiming to find the locking mechanism inside the lock itself and apply pressure to it. Once you've found it, pressing against the lock should pop the cuffs open.

59.

HOW TO ESCAPE FROM THE TRUNK OF A CAR

Ironically, this mainstay of crime dramas and gangster movies was rendered a little ineffective in the early 2000s, when internal emergency truck release switches began to be added to most vehicles. If that's not an option, however, you might need some luck, some brute force, or some ingenuity.

If you're in a car in which the rear seats can be lowered to gain access to the trunk, you may be able to kick or pry at least one of the seats down from within and force your way into the back seat.

Some models of cars have a switch to open the trunk next to the driver's seat too. You won't be able to reach that, but you may be able to access the cable that runs the length of the car and connects to the locking mechanism. Pull up the carpet lining the floor of the trunk or pry open the side panels to access the cable from within, and tug on it to release the lock.

If all else fails, you may need to attract other people's attention to help free you. Besides kicking and shouting, from inside the trunk, you may be able to gain access to the rear lights of the car, like the brake lights. Tear out their wires and push the bulb and covering out from within. Use the hole that is created to signal or call attention to your situation.

60.

HOW TO SURVIVE
A TORNADO

Tornados are nature's strongest storms, with winds reaching speeds of over 300mph. They can easily lift vehicles and implode buildings and are often accompanied by torrential rain and enormous hailstones. Surviving one, therefore, requires immediate action.

If you're indoors, keep away from any windows. Hide beneath a table or desk or protect yourself by wrapping something thick and padded around your body, like a quilt, blankets, or a sleeping bag. If possible, head to the smallest room on the lowest floor - or ideally, a windowless basement. Avoid tall buildings and buildings with broad flat roofs like gymnasiums.

If you're driving, you may well be able to outpace a tornado on open rural roads, but in built-up areas, your chances are slim. If your car is struck by debris or you see debris from the tornado being deposited on the road, it's time to pull over. Your car is a better shelter than no shelter at all, but its windows mean it is not ideal and broken glass may yet prove as dangerous as the storm itself. Keep your seatbelt fastened and hunker down as low as possible below the line of the window. Hold your hands over your head and neck. Use anything at your disposal to protect yourself from shattered glass.

If you're caught out in the open with no shelter at all, the trick is to get yourself as low as possible. Lying face down in a ditch or roadside verge, with your hands over the back of your head and neck, is your best bet.

61.

TOP 5 SURVIVAL HACKS: DENTAL FLOSS

Of all the things you might think to pack on a trip to the wilderness, dental floss probably isn't your most pressing concern. But in an emergency or survival situation, floss' light weight, strength, and waterproofness make it a useful stopgap in several different scenarios.

1. **AS TWINE.** You can use dental floss as a replacement for string, twine, or cord to lash together branches or posts to make the frame of a shelter or canoe, or to tie down a tarpaulin or plastic sheeting to form the roof of a shelter or the body of the boat. Braiding several strands of floss together will improve its strength and longevity.

2. **AS A TRIPWIRE.** Binding several strands of floss between two posts pushed into the ground will make an excellent tripwire for catching intruders, or tripping animals into a pit trap. Alternatively, encircle your camp with a strand of floss with metal cans or debris strung from it, to make an alarm system that will sound whenever anyone's foot catches in it.

3. **AS FISHING WIRE.** For hunting, you can use floss to fasten a blade to a pole to make a makeshift spear; bind

strands together to make the loop of a snare, or dangle a hook from a spool of floss to make a simple fishing wire.

4. **AS A CLOTHES WIRE.** String dental floss across your camp, tree to tree, to airdry your clothes quickly and safely. You can also use the same technique to suspend food supplies, keeping your next meal out of the way of the local wildlife.

5. **AS KINDLING.** Waxed dental floss burns well, so rolling it up into a loose ball makes excellent makeshift kindling for a campfire.

62.

HOW TO USE STONES
TO HEAT YOUR HOME

Once the wood or fuel of a fire burns out, the heat from the flames disappears instantly. The stones lining your campfire, however, will keep their heat for long afterwards -which is a trick worth knowing when it comes to heating your makeshift home or shelter.

Place a few large stones among the kindling and firewood of your fire before you light it. Do not place too many within the fire itself, however, as they can block the flow of oxygen, and as the firewood naturally collapses at it burns, they can break the fire up prematurely and cause it to go out. Once the fire has burned out, carefully extract the hot stones for your portable heat source.

Warming smoother, flatter stones like river rocks in the flames of a fire transforms them into a makeshift hot-water bottle too, ideal for slipping between your bedsheets in colder environments. You can also warm stones in a pan of water on the fire itself, and then as they cool, use them as heat pads to relax tight muscles after a hard day's work.

63.

HOW TO MAKE
A COMPASS

So long as you have a magnet - which these days can be found everywhere from your headphones to your mobile telephone - access to water, and a pin or some similarly thin piece of metal, you can make a compass.

Stroke the magnet a few dozen times along the pin, always in the same direction. Do not rub the magnet back and forth but lift it and reapply it between each stroke. Place the now magnetized need into a vessel of water - ideally floating atop something to support it, like a piece of cork - and it will naturally align itself north-south.

64.

HOW TO CATCH
A FISH

Essentially, there are three main methods of fishing: nets, rods, and spears. In a survival situation, chances are a fishing net isn't at hand, while making one from whatever natural resources you have at hand will either take too long or prove impossible. Fashioning a rod, hook, and a line is far simpler and quicker, and you are far more likely to have a twig, fiber, and metal pin or clip needed to make one.

Remember that fishing rods are flexible. Although a thick, strong, unbending timber might seem like the sensible choice, try to find a younger, greener stick that has a little give in it. Trim off any smaller offshoots, bend a paperclip or hairpin into a hook, and either use thread, vine, or dental floss as a makeshift line. Grubs, insects, and even small fruits can all be used as bait.

Spearfishing requires a keen eye as well as an ability to fashion a thicker, stronger, more robust timber into a point. Alternatively, use twine or floss to bind a knife to the end of a pole. One technique is to launch the pole into the water from the shore, which will let you cover more distance and apply more javelin-like power to the spear but will mean getting wet when you retrieve it afterwards. Alternatively, use a single longer spear to stab at shoals of fish from the shore; it'll be harder to control and won't give you as much purchase or strength, but at least you'll stay dry!

65.

HOW TO TIE A KNOT

Whether you're fixing a snapped shoelace or dangling from a rock face, knowing how to tie knots is a survival skill well worth knowing. There are as many different kinds of knots as there are situations in which you might need one, of course, but here are some of the basics.

An overhand knot is made by feeding the end of a rope back through a loop made in the same rope, producing a folded pretzel-shaped knot suitable for a handhold when climbing a rope.

Reef knots are simple binding knots used to link two ropes together or fasten something in place. Take the two ends and follow these simple instructions: right over left and under; left over right and through. In other words, lay the end in your right hand (A) over the end in your left hand (B), then fold the end of A under end B to form a cross-shaped knot. Tug on both ends to give yourself some slack, and then reverse the instructions again by passing A, now in your left hand, over B in your right. Pass B through the loop and tighten both ends to make a figure-eight-shaped knot.

Sheet bend knots too can be used to link two separate ropes together. Form a loop with one end (A), then feed the opposite end (B) through the loop, then under rope A, and then back through the loop in the opposite direction. Tighten the ropes to produce a bend knot linking the two together.

Lastly, bowline knots are useful climbing knots that make a strong loop in a rope that can be used as a handhold, foothold, or even around someone's chest or waist. Make two overlapping loops in the rope, like the loops of a rollercoaster. Pass the end of the rope back through both loops, then over and back under the loose rope on the other side, as if wrapping it up. Then pass the end back through the two loops, from the opposite side as before, and tighten it to produce a double bowline.

66.

HOW TO SURVIVE
AN AVALANCE

Avalanches can move at 200mph, and deposit hundreds of tons of snow in a matter of seconds. They are quite simply one of the most dangerous things you might encounter in the mountains. So, how can you ensure your survival?

If you've started the avalanche yourself by walking along a snowy mountainside, leap upward as soon as you feel the snow collapsing. If you're unlucky enough to be beneath the avalanche after it starts, you may still be able to escape by reacting quickly and moving to one side out of its path. Ditch any heavy equipment, and head toward the side of the oncoming avalanche.

If moving out of the way is not an option, grab onto something bigger and less movable than yourself, like a tree or a boulder. If these are strong enough to withstand the force that hits them, you'll have an anchor point from which to free yourself. This means you will likely not be buried as deeply as you would if you were knocked down the mountain on your own.

If the snow engulfs you, try to keep yourself upward and close to the surface as you fall to make your escape easier, and an air supply more accessible. Once the avalanche has stopped, dig as large a cavity as you can in front of your face to give you some breathing space. If you're able to, push your arm and hand upward above your head. If you can feel your hand reach out above the surface, you may be close enough to haul or "swim" your way free.

If you're utterly disorientated, spit a small amount of saliva out of your mouth; the direction that it flows under gravity will give you a sense of what direction you're lying in the snow. If you're unable to free yourself, keep calm and conserve air and energy while you await rescue.

67.

HOW TO TREAT
A GUNSHOT WOUND

Gunshot wounds are often bloody, so apply pressure to the wound to stem the flow of blood. Look for signs of shock – which can be caused by blood loss as well as trauma – and keep the victim comfortable and warm. Other than that, follow the basic tips for treating gunshot wounds: the A, B, C, D, Es.

A is for airway, and B is for breathing. If the person is conscious and speaking clearly, their airway is likely to be clear. Always check an unconscious person for any obstructions to their airway. Be careful, however, not to risk any sudden movements. If their breathing is erratic, slowing, or has stopped altogether, begin recovery CPR.

C is for circulation. Check the victim's pulse and stem any bleeding you can see. D is for disability. Assess any damage to the spinal column, head, or neck by asking the victim to move their extremities. If you suspect a serious injury, refrain from moving them in case you cause any further harm.

Lastly, E is for exposure: check for an exit wound, especially in a hard-to-see place like the back of the leg or the armpit.

As well as applying pressure to the wound itself, tying tourniquets around any major arteries nearby can help reduce blood loss. Applying pressure to the femoral artery in the thigh, for instance, can hold back blood supply to the whole limb and thereby reduce blood loss from a gunshot wound to the lower leg.

Chest wounds are trickier, as not only will they be bloody but if the bullet strikes a lung, air can escape through the wound, causing the lung to collapse. If a wound is foaming or sucking, or the victim is wheezing or coughing up blood, apply pressure to the chest wound and ideally form a seal over it using impermeable material, like soft plastic. Leave a small gap in the seal to allow oxygen to escape and maintain pressure until the emergency services arrive.

68.

HOW TO RESTART
A HEART

They're two terms often used interchangeably, but a heart attack and cardiac arrest are not the same things.

In a heart attack, blood flow to the heart is blocked. In cardiac arrest, the heart malfunctions and stops beating altogether, and as a result, oxygen-rich blood flows to the rest of the body ceases. A heart attack can lead to a person going into cardiac arrest, but the two are identical.

CPR - cardiopulmonary resuscitation - effectively mimics the natural movement of the heart from the outside by forcing blood out of the heart and circulating it around the body, essentially doing its job for it.

To give CPR, push down hard and fast in the middle of a person's chest with your hands, at a rate of around 100–120 beats per minute (the tempo of the Bee Gees song "Stayin' Alive"). Every 40 pushes, tip the patient's head back, grasp the chin and open the mouth then blow twice forcefully into the patient's mouth to keep their oxygen levels as high as possible. Keep the CPR going until emergency care arrives.

The purpose of CPR is not to restart a stopped heart, however, but only to continue doing its job for it until more invasive medical help arrives. To restart a stopped heart and restore its natural rhythm, you would need an AED - an automated external defibrillator. First aid has advanced enough that these electronic devices can now be found everywhere from gyms to shopping malls. They carry clear and concise instructions for when and how they should be used.

69.

TOP FIVE SURVIVAL HACKS: MOBILE PHONE

Your battery may be dead, or the network may be down, but your cell phone can still be useful in a survival situation. Here are five reasons why.

1. **AS A HELIOGRAPH.** A heliograph is a method of reflecting or shining a glimmer of sunlight to signal to someone else. Most modern smartphones have a full smooth glass front, which in an emergency can be used to do precisely that. Point the glass at the sun, and then shine the reflected beam at whoever you're trying to get the attention of and hopefully the glimmering light will catch their eye.

2. **AS A COMPASS.** Most smartphones have a compass app these days, but if your phone is well and truly wrecked, you can use the magnets in your phone's speakers to make a simple compass. Stroke the magnet along a ferrous wire a dozen or so times to charge it, then let it float in a pool of water. It will naturally align itself north to south.

3. **TO START A FIRE.** Your phone's battery might still carry enough charge to spark a fire, either by holding it against

steel wool, or by using the same foil technique outlined earlier.

4. **AS A CUTTING TOOL.** If you've ever dropped your phone and shattered the glass screen, you'll be painfully aware that its glass cover is eminently breakable. Use a glass shard as a simple cutting tool; use larger shards to tip spears or to make knives; or use the metal backing to fashion into prongs, forks, or similar implements.

5. **AS BINOCULARS.** If your phone isn't dead, of course, there's still plenty you can do with it, some more practical than others. Smartphone cameras are so impressively accurate these days that in place of a pair of binoculars, you can take a photo of the landscape you want to see in more detail, then zoom in on the picture to take a closer look without ever lifting your head.

70.

HOW TO SURVIVE
BEING LOST AT SEA

If you're alone in the water, perhaps with only a life jacket to help you, your priority is to get back to shore. Luckily, the chances of you being alone in the open ocean without any kind of vessel like that are slim; chances are, you've just become detached from your surfboard or paddleboard, and so will likely be within reachable distance of land.

If you know your way back, try to swim or float back toward the shore. If you're wearing a floatation device, swimming on your back may be easier; you may even find deflating it slightly gives you better control in the water. If you find yourself being swept toward rocks, try to position yourself feet first in the water to cushion the impact.

If you're completely lost at sea in a boat, however, finding the direction of the nearest shore is imperative. Keep an eye out for changes in water color (shallower water is usually paler), floating debris (leaves are a good sign of nearby land), and seabirds. The wind will typically blow toward land during the day, and off the land and across the sea at night too.

With no land in sight, rescue is your main chance of survival, in which case you may have to do what you can to endure several days or even weeks at sea. Do not discard anything; you have no idea how useful even the most throwaway items may be with nothing else around you. Do not drink seawater, but fashion some way of collecting rainwater if possible. Dehydration will be more of a pressing problem than hunger, but finding food is nevertheless important. Use anything you can - from torn-up clothing to the toecaps of shoes - to fashion fishing lines and hooks. Remember, you may have to use smaller, inedible fish as bait to catch larger ones.

71.

HOW TO STOP A CAR
WITH NO BRAKES

When, where, and how you discover your moving car has no brakes will determine how best you can safely bring it to a halt.

If you're driving a car with a manual gearbox, you can gradually "downshift" it to a stop. Dropping the car into the next gear down will force it to work harder to maintain its current speed, causing it to slow. Repeat the process down through the remaining gears, until you're going slow enough to either manually break the car or ditch it safely by the roadside.

If all else fails, you might need to take more practical action. Opening the car windows increases drag, and so can be used at a pinch to take a few mph off your speed. Look out for inclines or slopes, which will naturally knock some pace out of your vehicle too.

As a last resort, "dragging" the car involves gently nudging it to the side of the road and knocking it against a wall or roadside barrier. Judge this carefully, though, and approach the barrier at a glancing angle - you're only trying to take the pace out of the car, not crash it.

If all of this happens on a busy stretch of road, of course, make sure other drivers know you're having a problem. Turn on your hazard lights and move to the side of the road or to the curbside verge.

72.

HOW TO OPEN A CAN
WITHOUT A CAN OPENER

Here's a fact that proves we humans aren't the best at doing forward planning: the can opener was invented 48 years after the metal can itself!

So, what did people do in those intervening years? Or, to put it another way, what if you find yourself in a situation where you desperately need to open a can but have no opener at hand?

If you're lucky enough to have a sharp knife, one thing not to try is to saw the lid of the can off as if the knife were a can opener. That can blunt the knife, damage the can, and leave sharp metal shavings in your food.

Instead, with one hand, hold the knife vertically, with the tip of the blade pointing downward against the lid of the can, just inside the lid. With the flat of your other hand, slap down sharply on the handle of the night, aiming to pierce the tip of the blade through the metal lid. You may need to anchor the can in place to stop it from skittering away - though best not to clamp it between your thighs, for obvious reasons...

Continue piercing a circle of slits around the inside edge of the can. There's no need to join these together in one long opening;

essentially perforating the can with a series of slits might make it weak enough to then be pried off using the blade.

At a push (quite literally), the tip of a spoon can be jimmied into the edge of the lip of a can too to make an opening, or you can try to abrade the can against a rough surface, like a stone or a concrete block, until enough of the metal has been rubbed away to pry it open.

73.

HOW TO SURVIVE
LOSING A LIMB

Injuring yourself far from help is bad enough, but losing a limb is a nightmarish scenario. So, no matter whether it's an industrial machinery mishap, an encounter with a wild animal, or a *127 Hours*-style freak accident, how can you treat an inadvertent amputation when professional medical care is not an option?

Your number one priority is to stem the loss of blood. Your legs and arms are served by your femoral and brachial arteries, severing either of which could lead to catastrophic blood loss in a matter of minutes. Elevate the affected limb and apply pressure to the wound to stem the flow. Then, if necessary, use a tourniquet or a similar binding to close off as many of the nearby blood vessels as possible. If the detached limb is salvageable and you're not too far from help, it may still be able to be reattached, so do not leave it behind if emergency care is possible.

Once the bleeding has slowed, wrap the wound in a sterile dressing or clean fabric if possible. If the blood still soaks through, apply another dressing over the top without removing the first - doing so may disturb the wound further, and restart the slowed bleeding. Only in extreme circumstances should more dramatic procedures be undertaken: a large limb loss wound that does not stop bleeding, for instance, can be cauterized with metal heated in the flames of a fire.

74.

HOW TO CRACK
A SAFE

It sounds like a Hollywood trope, but you can actually use a stethoscope to listen to the intricate mechanism inside a safe and crack it open. It's a difficult process, nonetheless, and professional locksmiths take many years to attune their ears to the precise combination of sounds they're looking for as the delicate cogs inside the combination lock fall into place.

It's a method too detailed to go into fully in this book, but here are the basics.

Inside a combination lock are a series of toothed wheels, each of which corresponds to a number in the safe's combination. A three-digit code (like 12-34-56) would have three wheels, for instance; a 99-digit lock, however, will have millions of possible combinations, so guessing even a three-digit code would require more time than you would ever have available.

If you don't know how many wheels the lock has (or digits the combination has), you'll need to first figure that out by listening out for a series of clicks as one of the wheels slides into position inside the lock and begins to pick up the second wheel behind it, and so on. Once you've ascertained the length of the code, you'll need to begin figuring out the code, utilizing trial and error - and lots of patience - to listen out for the same series of gentle clicks as each digit of the combination slides into place.

It's easy to mishear what's going on, and it's easy to get lost in your counting, so you may find writing the digits down and keeping track of your progress on paper helpful. Eventually, your counting and listening will align, and the lock will snap into place.

75.

HOW TO ESCAPE
FROM ZIP TIES

Let's not dwell on *how* you've ended up with a plastic zip tie around your wrists, let's just try to get you out of them.

With no one around to cut you free, you're either going to have to find an equally sharp object against which to rub the ties to snap them or manipulate your body to yield enough force to split them apart. And to do that, you're going to have to tighten - yes, tighten - the ties as much as possible. That will stretch and weaken the plastic, while the added pressure is going to make popping the ties off your hands much easier. So, tug at the loose end of the tie with your teeth to increase the tension around your wrist as much as you can.

If your arms are free, raise your bound hands above your head with your palms facing inward, toward one another. As quickly as possible, bring your arms forcibly downward, and at the same time thrust your midriff forward. The two forces coming together should impart enough force to push your hands apart, safely snapping the zip tie as they go.

76.

HOW TO SURVIVE
A SPIDER BITE

All spiders are capable of biting, but spider bites themselves can range from itchy minor irritations to potentially fatal injuries.

Wash the area with mild soap and cool water. Use an ice pack to chill the site of the bite and reduce inflammation. This will help stem the flow of venom throughout your system. Elevating a bitten hand or leg can also help slow the spread of the venom, as can fastening a tourniquet-like bandage tightly around the affected part.

If possible, capture or at least identify the spider that has bitten you - but only if doing so does not risk another bite. Medical professionals will need to know what antivenom to administer, so knowing precisely what has bitten you will ensure prompt treatment.

Keep a watchful eye for any signs of a serious bite, like fever, chills, body aches, vomiting, or itchy or painful discoloration of the wound. Any of these might hint at the spider bite being more serious than first anticipated and would demand immediate emergency medical care.

77.

HOW TO REMOVE
YOUR OWN APPENDIX

In 1961, Soviet doctor Leonid Rogozov was spending the long winter months at an Antarctic research station when his appendix suddenly flared up. Rogozov was the station's only doctor, and so his incapacitation (or worse) was not an option. There was no one else on the base to assist him, so he had to do the all-but-unimaginable: perform abdominal surgery on himself and remove his own appendix! The self-operation took two hours, but astonishingly, he survived. The freak occurrence has since led to the urban legend that people visiting Antarctica need to have had their appendix removed - in fact, it is merely anyone who wants to serve as a doctor there.

So perhaps, like Leonid Rogozov, you're trapped in the middle of nowhere, you suddenly develop appendicitis, and you are unable to get to the emergency room. The pain in your abdomen is excruciating, and your appendix is close to rupturing, making potentially fatal peritonitis a real and present danger. Regardless of where you are, you're going to have to get rid of that offending organ. So, how can you do it?

Let's be honest, this isn't a procedure for the fainthearted, nor indeed for the medically uninitiated; if it were, chances are one of the Antarctic scientists would have stepped in to help. So, even though you may be able to access the appendix and cut it free to stave off peritonitis, this story is far from over: emergency medical care would be imperative to ensure the wound is properly sealed, bleeding stemmed, and infections kept at bay.

Hopefully, you at least have a sharp knife at hand, and some medical-grade suturing thread. You'll need to make a 2–4-inch incision on the lower right-hand side of your abdomen, directly above the site of your appendix, slightly below the line formed by your hip bone and navel.

You'll need to cut down some distance through your subcutaneous fat and abdominal muscles to expose the peritoneum - the membrane-like lining of the abdomen - and the intestine beneath. Locating the appendix is not easy, but you're looking for a pouch-like appendage, connected by a thin, translucent membrane to the underside of the intestinal tube. If possible, tie off the neck of the appendix with a loop of suturing thread, before cutting the organ free.

There is a mass of blood vessels in this region, all of which in a proper surgery would be clamped shut to avoid loss of blood. Stitching the wound closed, ultimately, is not the end of the story and a trip to the hospital - now sans appendix - is absolutely imperative.

78.

HOW TO SURVIVE
AN EARTHQUAKE

The basic advice for seeing out an earthquake is to drop, cover, and hold on.

If you're indoors, move away from any glass, overhanging lights or lamps, shelves, or anything else that could cause injury if shaken free. Drop low to the ground and find some shelter - under a sturdy table is ideal, but at a push crouching in the interior corner of a building will suffice. Use your hands - or ideally a pillow or cushion - to protect your head and neck from falling debris and remain in place until the shaking stops.

If you're outdoors, do the opposite: do *not* head for cover, but see wide open spaces, away from tall trees, high walls, buildings, lampposts, utility poles, and power lines. If you're driving, likewise stop in a clear area away from any structures, in particular bridges or overpasses.

79.

HOW TO SURVIVE
A TSUNAMI

Despite being better known as tidal waves, tsunamis are not caused by the action of the tide, but by underwater earthquakes that rupture the seabed and create enormous waves that can sweep onto nearby land. That makes them utterly devastating disasters but at least gives those on land a few much-needed minutes to respond and move to safety.

Move to higher ground - the higher, the better. Areas that are prone to tsunamis not only tend to have designated tsunami warning systems but tsunami evacuation routes that should direct you to your nearest area of high land.

If you're in a building and do not have time to evacuate, move to a higher floor or - even better if the building is sturdy enough - onto the roof. If all else fails, climb the nearest tall tree you can find.

As well as moving upward, you'll ideally want to move inward, inland away from the coast. Tsunamis can sweep water and debris several miles inland, but their power lessens as the waves break against buildings and undulating ground, so inland is much safer than the coast.

If the worst happens and you're swept away, debris in the water is an immediate danger - but it can also offer you a chance to escape. Cling on to something buoyant and sturdy, like wood or the bough of a tree, and try to ride out the waters as best you can. The entire process may well be over in a matter of minutes, so hold on and try to see it out.

80.

HOW TO FREE YOURSELF FROM A STRAITJACKET

Houdini could do it, so why shouldn't you?

Straitjackets hold your arms in place folded across your lower torso. So, when one is put on you, you need to ensure your stronger dominant hand and arm are on the outside. As the jacket is being tightened, stand up straight, take a deep breath, and if possible, surreptitiously grab some of the fabric from the inside and bunch it together in your hand. Doing all of these will mean the jacket is tightened in such a way that you will actually have some slack and some leeway inside even once it is fastened.

To begin your escape, drop your chest and shoulders as if slouching, to make your body as small as possible. With the leeway you have created, begin edging your dominant hand past your weaker arm and up toward your opposite shoulder. Keep your hand on your shoulder and pass your head through the crook of your elbow.

Once through, you should be able to move both of your hands and arms more freely. Then you can use your teeth to undo the buckles and straps of the jacket to complete your escape!

81.

HOW TO BUILD
A SHELTER

After food and water, the one thing you're going to need in any survival situation is shelter from the elements. Depending on where you are and what equipment you have at your disposal, your shelter may be more comfortable and more permanent than others, but as a rough guide, a basic tent-like structure can be erected fairly easily.

First things first, location is everything. Find an area of level ground that is not too wet or boggy, nor too overgrown; the more undergrowth you have to clear, the less time, natural light, and energy you'll have to build your new home. Be mindful of slopes that could make you susceptible to landslips or see your shelter flooded out in bad weather. Building your shelter by a lake, a river, or the coast may seem like a good idea too, but such areas are always popular with wildlife - so choose wisely based on what kinds of creatures you know to dwell nearby.

Next, create a frame by binding or interlocking sturdy poles, posts, or branches. Simpler shelters can be built in a wigwam style, with the poles coming together at a single central point; others that are larger and more complex can be built around A-frames, though they would require more effort and materials to construct efficiently.

If you have plastic sheeting or tarpaulin to cover the shelter, remember too to secure it against the ground to stop it from blowing away. You can drive pegs into the ground to pin or tie the tarp down, or simply weigh it down with earth or stones. If you don't have any premade roof at hand, broad leaves and even tree branches with densely packed leaves can provide enough cover to keep your shelter waterproof.

82.

HOW TO DRY OUT WOOD FOR BURNING

A good woodworker knows that drying or "seasoning" freshly hewn wood will make it stronger and better to work with. In a survival situation, however, like building a campfire, your priority is not to find wood to build with but that is dry enough to burn (without producing clouds of dense black smoke). The problem is that local weather conditions might not exactly be conducive to that, of course, so how can you dry out the wood you have available to make it suitable?

Leaving wood out in hot sunshine will remove at least some of its moisture but often not enough for it to burn efficiently. To speed up the drying process, build a frame to keep your wood off the wet ground and to allow air to circulate all around it. Split or cut your firewood down into smaller pieces, so that as much of the damp interior of the wood is exposed as possible. Rather than merely quartering a log, for instance, cut each quarter down in smaller shards that will dry faster than larger blocks.

If you have longer-term plans, find a cool, dry place in which to store your wood and ideally leave it for several weeks or even months to dry out completely. Plan ahead: cut your firewood early enough in the year so that sufficient is prepared in time for the colder months. Always overestimate how much you will need; better to have plenty of wood left over by spring than run out while there is still snow on the ground.

83.

HOW TO ESCAPE
AN UPSIDE-DOWN VEHICLE

If you're in an accident and feel your car is about to flip or roll over, remove your feet from the pedals to prevent injury to your ankles. Let go of the steering wheel and hold your arms across your chest and press back into the seat to brace yourself.

Once the vehicle has stopped rolling, turn off the engine. Try to remain calm as you assess yourself and your passengers for injury. As well as broken bones, injuries from flying shattered glass are possible, some of which may be difficult to see amidst hair or clothing.

To exit an upturned vehicle, brace your feet against the floor and your arms against the roof. You're going to have to undo your seatbelt while experiencing a seated handstand, supporting your weight as best you can. If you don't brace yourself correctly, you could drop out of your seat headfirst. So long as you're supporting your weight effectively, you should be able to gradually lower yourself from your seat and crawl free.

If the windows have shattered, do not try to use the door as it may be supporting the car's weight; instead, crawl free through the window frame, being mindful of the glass. Once you're free, assist any passengers in freeing themselves, then move away from the vehicle in case of a potentially explosive fuel leak.

84.

HOW TO BOOST
YOUR PHONE SIGNAL

In the middle of nowhere, finding a sufficient mobile phone signal to call for help can be tricky, but can make the difference between being found and being lost.

To improve your signal, you'll want to find as open and as elevated an area as possible. Avoid buildings, trees, power lines, electric lights, and other electronic devices, all of which can disrupt a digital signal. Remember too that signals can "bounce" off obstacles, so although you may be standing in open ground, depending on the location of your nearest cell tower, the signal may be struggling to work its way around a billboard or a water tower.

Phones rarely have obvious aerials anymore, but the principle is still the same. Inside the receiver is an antenna, which needs to be pointed upright to find a solid signal.

Smartphone batteries are sometimes programmed to withhold battery power in case you need to make or receive a call, often at the expense of finding a solid signal. Even if the signal appears weak or nonexistent on your phone's screen, ultimately, it may be worthwhile attempting a call to see if the extra boost of power in doing that forces your phone to summon up helps it find a connection too.

85.

HOW TO FIND
WHICH WAY IS NORTH

If you're not looking at the stars or building a makeshift compass (look elsewhere in this book for tips on those), what other methods are there for ascertaining which way is north?

Folklore will have you believe that moss only grows on the north side of trees (nope, sorry), and that certain livestock will always orient themselves along a north-south line (nope, that's a myth too). Instead, if you're out in the open unsure of which way to head, all you need is some sunlight, a sturdy twig, an area of open ground, and a few rocks.

Find a twig that is strong enough to remain standing when pushed into the ground. So long as you're out in the open, the upright twig will cast a shadow. Mark the end of the shadow with a rock.

Wait 15–20 minutes. As the sun moves across the sky, the tip of the shadow will shift with it. Mark its new location with a second rock. Draw a line in the earth connecting the two.

Because the sun moves from east to west, the second shadow - and thereby the second rock - will be cast further east than the first. The line you've drawn between the two, ultimately, is an east-west line, which you can then use easily to orient yourself.

86.

HOW TO NAVIGATE USING THE STARS

With even a cursory knowledge of the constellations, you can easily find north, south, east, and west.

In the northern hemisphere, use Ursa Minor, the Little Bear (AKA the Big Dipper, or the Plough), to find the north. It's that familiar constellation that looks like a four-pointed box, with a long handle-like tail extending from it. The last and brightest star in the tail is Polaris, the Pole Star or North Star, which lies less than 1° off due north.

Extend your arm to its full extent and clench your fist. Stack your hands, fist atop fist, from the horizon to the North Star. Each fist will equate to roughly 10° latitude and can give you a vague approximation of your position from the equator without the need for a sextant or quadrant.

In the southern hemisphere, you'll want to look for the constellation *Crux*, or the Southern Cross, a simple +-shaped constellation comprising four stars. Then look to a point in the night sky on the left of the South Cross, roughly four times the distance between its left and right points. That, roughly speaking, is due south.

87.

HOW TO LIGHT
A WET MATCH

You can spark a match in innumerable ways, but if the match is wet, the task becomes a lot harder. You can, of course, manufacture a flame in some way, like concentrating the light of the sun onto the head of the match using a magnifying glass or a lens of some kind.

Alternatively, you need to improve your chances of getting the match to spark somehow. One method is to strike several matches at once. Another is to rub the entire match - not just the matchhead - flat against a rough surface, like a piece of sandpaper, a concrete block, or a piece of wood. Rubbing the wood of the match will naturally help to dry it, but by increasing the amount of the matchhead being rubbed in this way, the single match alone has a better chance of sparking even when wet.

88.

HOW TO ESCAPE
A RIP CURRENT

Rip tides can be dangerous and frightening if you're caught in one, but with a level head and by taking evasive action, you can still escape.

If the water in the rip current is not too deep, attempt to stand rather than swim. You'll have to brace yourself, but with enough purchase on the sea floor, you may be able to slowly wade your way back to shore. If the water is too deep to find your feet, however, you'll have to swim. Do not attempt to swim *through* the current, but swim *parallel* to it.

That may well mean swimming parallel to the shore, rather than toward it, but by maintaining a safe position behind the current, you'll be able to work your way along it. If you begin to tire, don't panic, or force yourself to keep going, but tread water for a minute or so until you catch your breath. As you work your way down the current, you'll eventually feel it slacken as the seabed changes. Once it does, you should be able to swim your way back to shore or allow yourself to drift in closer on breaking waves.

89.

HOW TO TREAT
SUNBURN

In an ideal situation, you'd treat sunburn with medicated ointments and specialized creams. In a survival situation, you might not have quite so robust a medicine cabinet. So, what else can you do?

Use water and a cloth to cool the affected skin. As your skin repairs itself, you can help it along from the inside by keeping yourself hydrated too. That will help to lower your body temperature, keep your blood flowing, and keep your skin hydrated as it heals.

There are plenty of natural remedies for sunburn, access to which will depend on where you find yourself. Adding vinegar, baking soda, oatmeal, and even chamomile tea to the water used to soothe the affected skin has all long been touted as effective natural remedies. But if you're stuck in a desert landscape, your best bet is an aloe plant, the soothing gel of which is so effective that even over-the-counter sunburn creams often contain it.

90.

HOW TO ESCAPE
FROM QUICKSAND

Quicksand isn't quite as dangerous as it's often portrayed in the movies but finding yourself trapped and sinking in loose earth is still a perilous situation - especially if you're out hiking alone in the wilderness. Although the quicksand itself may not be as perilous as you think, being trapped in mud when a tide comes in or being unable to move to shelter when a storm approaches, can quickly prove fatal.

First of all, do not panic. It takes a few seconds for quicksand to liquefy, but panicked, thrashing movements and flailing limbs will speed up that process and loosen the ground faster than slower, more deliberate movements. If you're able to, try to wiggle out of your shoes. The flatter soles of shoes and boots will naturally create suction on wet or loose ground, whereas the smoother natural arch of your foot will not.

Drop or throw aside anything that's weighing you down. Lightening the load will decrease the downward pressure you're imparting on the ground.

If you're standing upright, all of your bodyweight is pressing down on your two feet, so lean back or forward to spread your weight over a larger area. In shallow quicksand, this alone might be enough to soften the mud around your feet and free yourself (albeit at the expense of dirtying your clothes), while in deeper quicksand, as the mud loosens you might be able to roll or "swim" your way to safety.

Remember, most quicksand is only a few feet deep, so the chances of you sinking completely are slim. Not dealing with the situation correctly, however, can easily see you trapped to above your knees, waist, or even chest relatively quickly, all of which will make your eventual escape all the more difficult.

91.

HOW TO MAKE
A WHISTLE

When you're lost in the wilderness, anything that attracts attention to your plight will come in handy. That may well include making your own whistle.

Simple whistles can be made either from clay - producing a round, handheld ocarina-style instrument - or from hollow reeds or sticks, with fingerholes bored into them to produce a pennywhistle-style instrument. If you're not so bothered about playing a tune but simply making a sound, however, you can make a fairly effective handheld whistle out of an old soda can.

The pliable, crushable metal of a drink can make it ideal for this. Cut two strips of metal from the can, both of equal width, but one twice as long as the other. Lay the shorter piece of the longer piece to make a crucifix-like cross. Then fold over the sides of the shorter piece so that they cling on to the longer one. Next, fold the end of the longer piece down over the two folded sides of the shorter piece, and curl the free end around to make a semicircle. The entire whistle should now resemble an open P-shape.

Cut a hole in the flat folded edge of the whistle to make a mouthpiece. Open the hole slightly, and you're ready to blow!

92.

HOW TO READ A MAP

When it comes to looking at a map and attempting to navigate, it can all become something of a confusing blur. Here are some basics to keep you on track.

Although some regional maps use square grids as a simple A1, B2, and C3-style means of showing the location of things, the gridwork on larger-scale maps typically shows latitude and longitude. Both are measured in degrees, with horizontal latitude lines showing distance north or south of the equator, and vertical longitude lines showing the distance from the 0° Greenwich meridian.

The wavier, often brown-colored lines used on more detailed maps of smaller locations are known as contour lines and show the height of the land in a given location above sea level. The more densely packed the lines are drawn, the steeper the incline you can expect, so when it comes to planning a hike, used these lines to figure out how challenging a trip you can expect.

It's tempting to think maps will be drawn with north at the top and south at the bottom, but often regional maps are aligned slightly off center for the benefit of orienting the landscape sensibly. All maps will typically show due north relative to how they are laid out somewhere on the paper.

Maps are scaled according to distance; depending on how detailed or zoomed-in a map may be, you can usually expect anything around an inch to equate anything from several hundred feet to a few miles. To measure the distance of a track or a journey, use a piece of string to plot out your route and mark your finishing point. Then hold the string flat against the scale as it is printed on the map, or for longer distances, measure the length of the string from start to finish and multiply accordingly.

93.

HOW TO BOAT
DOWN RAPIDS

Finding your way down any watercourse can be difficult, but when the water starts to foam and turn into rapids, you'll have quite a challenge on your hands.

A handy acronym for navigating rapids is WORMS - water, obstacles, route, markers, and safety.

Keep an eye on the nature of the water ahead, and look out for eddying currents, cascades, sudden drops, or plunge pools. Try to discern where the most forceful water is flowing, and either paddle clear of it, or lift your paddles and ride it out.

Look ahead for obstacles too, like boulders and fallen trees that might damage your boat or entangle you. Envisage your best route. Markers are visible landmarks like trees, bridges, rocks, and so on that, you can use to keep track of your progress downstream. And keep your safety paramount: if a route looks impassable or too dangerous, it may well be a better option to head to the shore and carry your boat further downstream before rejoining the river at a later point.

94.

HOW TO SHARPEN A KNIFE

At home in the kitchen, all manner of gadgetry can be used to sharpen your knives, but out on the road or in the wilderness, you may not be quite so spoilt for choice. What's more, cutting with a blunt knife can be more dangerous than using a sharp one, as you must apply more pressure to cut, and that extra effort may cause the knife to slip uncontrollably.

To sharpen a knife, you need a whetstone. Some survival kits and outdoor kits these days include portable, synthetic whetstones, which are classified according to their "grit" - that is, the coarseness of the stone, with coarser grits used on larger tools like axes, and smaller grits used on pocket knives. If you have no such stone available, you'll have to find yourself a flattened rock with not too coarse a grain on which to sharpen your blade.

Keep the whetstone slightly damp or lubricated with mineral oil to make for a smooth pass and to avoid damaging the blade further. Then hold the blade at roughly a 20° angle to the stone and pull down, gently passing the length of the blade against the stone to grind away the dull edge. Flip the knife over and repeat it on the other side until you have a new symmetrical edge to the blade that has been formed.

95.

HOW TO SAFELY
TRANSPORT FUEL

You are part of a convoy, and one car breaks down. There's a garage some miles ahead, so you carry on driving to go fetch some fuel. But how can you safely transport that fuel back to your awaiting companion?

Let's make no bones about it: it is extremely dangerous to transport fuel in a vehicle.

Not only is the fuel itself flammable, but as the liquid is jostled around, it can create a vapor that is very easily sparked by even the smallest of ignitions.

Fuel should always be carried in a suitable container, not liable to degrade, and fitted with a tight seal. Ideally, it should not be transported in another open vehicle at all (and different territories have different rules about the amount of fuel - if any - private individuals are permitted to carry), but in an emergency you may have no other option. Only carry as much as you need and be fully aware at all times of how dangerous a cargo you're transporting.

96.

HOW TO STERILIZE
A WOUND

No matter how successfully you treat a wound in the wild unless the wound is kept clean and sterile, it can easily become infected - which in some cases can prove an even greater emergency than the wound itself.

If your first aid kid has sterile wipes, swaps, or liquid alcohol, clean *around* the wound effectively. If those are not available, fresh clean water is an appropriate (though not ideal) replacement.

That being said, any water that is good enough to drink can be used to clean *inside* the wound perfectly well. A plastic syringe is an ideal tool for directing a jet of fresh water into a cut to swill out any foreign matter and keep it clean.

Remember, you can also use clean boiling water to sterilize first aid kit tools - like knives, scissors, and tweezers - both before and after use.

97.

TOP FIVE SURVIVAL HACKS: SIGNAL FOR HELP

When you're lost in the wilderness, attracting enough attention to yourself to be found or rescued is imperative. If you've thought ahead, you might have packed a few pieces of kit that could help with precisely that - but if not, you're going to have to improvise.

1. **MAKE A NOISE.** It should go without saying that shouting for help is an ideal start when it comes to ensuring rescue. When your voice gives out, however, you can always improvise and make a whistle, or bang on trees or solid ground to make a thunderous sound that can be heard over quite some distance.

2. **HARNESS THE SUN.** Reflective surfaces like shards of glass, kitchen foil, metal drinks containers, and even makeup mirrors can all be used to make heliographs - devices that reflect the sun, producing a flickering, dazzling signal that can be seen over quite some distance. Essentially, you're making your own sun-powered lighthouse, so the larger and more reflective the surface you can make the better.

3. **LIGHT A BEACON.** Find yourself on high ground and build your campfire. Your fire should be burning away

from trees and foliage anyway, but in a search-and-rescue situation, the more isolated your fire is, the more visible it can be. Don't dismiss lighting a fire during the daytime either - the smoke will be even more visible than the flames.

4. **WRITE A MESSAGE.** Chances are if people are looking for you, they'll be doing so at some point from the air. Use rocks, timbers, debris, or anything else at your disposal to make a sign that will be visible from the air. It doesn't have to be a full-on message - any non-random shape, like a circle or a triangle, will attract attention from the air so long as it is visible and sizable enough.

5. **USE COLOUR.** When it comes to keeping things visible, utilize every bit of colored kit you have. If you have a bright red backpack, empty it out and use the bright red fabric as a signal. The brighter and more unusual colors you can track down, the more likely you are to be noticed.

98.

HOW TO MAKE
A ROPE SWING

Depending on the context, a rope swing is either a fun backyard project for a lazy summer weekend or a means of transporting yourself or your kit across a river or ravine in safety. Either way, you'll need a rope and some kind of base on which to sit or from which to hang your belongings.

For your seat, you need a strong timber roughly 2–3 feet long by 4–6 inches long. The flatter the better, but strength rather than comfort is your top priority.

Bore a hole at either corner and fasten through a loop of rope on either end. Tie off the rope underneath the swing and use a match or taper to singe the loose threads of the rope to stop it from unravelling. Use can use supporting timbers beneath the seat to strengthen it, or to shore up the holes through which the rope is looped.

To make a swing, all you need do is loop both ropes over a strong enough tree branch. To use the same mechanism more practically, you can hook the loops over a third rope slung across a river or similar divide and haul yourself and your across.

99.

HOW TO SURVIVE
A LONG FALL

You've taken a tumble down a mountainside. So, what next?

As long as you're not falling into thin air, try to break your fall up by reaching out for whatever handhold or foothold you can find - like protruding boulders or branches. You might not stop yourself from falling, but you might slow your descent enough to make survival more likely.

Try not to panic and tense your body up. Instead, keep yourself loose - the so-called "ragdoll effect" - so that your body absorbs each impact. If you can see the end of the fall below you, try to right yourself so that you land feet first, and keep your knees slightly bent to absorb the final impact.

You may land on your feet, but if your fall was a rapid one, you likely won't stop moving. Your feet and legs may have absorbed the impact, but you'll likely fall and then bounce. The bounce is often just as dangerous as the fall itself, and many people who find themselves in similar situations survive the first descent relatively unscathed, only to hit or land on their head when they rebound.

So, if possible, control your bounce by falling to the side, or straight forward, cushioning yourself with your arms. Try not to fall backward, as that can make protecting your head difficult.

100.

HOW TO PICK A LOCK

So far, we've escaped from a locked room and a pair of handcuffs. But what about a simple tumbler lock, of the kind that's often used on padlocks?

Inside a tumbler lock is a row of spring-loaded pins - anywhere from three to eight in a standard lock - which the bumpy teeth of the key, known as the ward, push upward to open it. If a lock has become rusted or decayed, you may need to spray a lubricant into the lock to help ease the mechanism into action before you begin.

To prize the lock open, you'll need a tension wrench and a pick. The tension wrench is designed to push down into the shaft of the lock, known as the keyway, making room for the pick to push the pins out of the way. You won't be able to see what you're doing, of course, but having an idea of what you're working with will make the task easier to envisage. Note also that some locks - especially in Europe - are the other way up, so you'll have to push upward with the tension wrench, and downward against the pins.

If you don't have professional tools, you'll have to make a suitable wrench and pick from whatever you have available. Paperclips and bobby pins work perfectly well.

While applying pressure to the keyway using the wrench, insert your pick and begin lifting the pins inside the lock gently, one at a time. Applying too much force may cause the lock to freeze, and you'll have to reset the mechanism to open it. With all the pins gradually lifted free, turn the wrench in the same direction you would a key, and the lock should click open.

101.

HOW TO START
A FIRE

We've dealt with building a campfire safely, starting a fire with a cell phone battery and a broken lightbulb, and even using damp matches. But how else can you start a fire?

It's a childhood trick but harnessing the sun with a magnifying lens is a neat way of focusing a beam of hot light onto kindling and causing it to spark. Striking the edge of a flint stone - ideally with a piece of high-carbon metal, like steel - should cause a spark large enough to catch alight too. Holding steel wool to the terminals of a nine-volt battery will cause it to catch fire, and you shouldn't ignore good old friction too. You can use a small bow-like tool, looped around a vertical pole, to rotate the pole swiftly enough to produce heat and, ultimately, burn the kindling.

102.

HOW TO GET HONEY
FROM A BEEHIVE

If you're lucky, you might well stumble across a natural beehive out in the wilderness. More likely than not, however, you'll have to search for one, by following the flightpaths of bees through the air, and listening out as their buzzing becomes louder.

Once you've located a hive, however, how can you safely extract its honey? Just like professional beekeepers, you'll want to produce smoke. Burn something like green grass, plants, or pine needles to produce a lot of dense smoke and waft it into the entrance to the hive. The smoke will disorientate the bees, and while they are distracted, you can use a sharp knife to carve away part of the hive and harvest the honey. To stay safe, keep your movements slow and deliberate; do not bat or thrash at the bees, and certainly do not squash them like any old bug. More importantly, however, don't get too greedy and demolish too much of the hive. Not only will that ruin your newfound supply, but the bees may well angrily pursue the remnants of their home, giving you an entirely new set of problems to deal with!

103.

HOW TO MAKE SALTWATER DRINKABLE

Unless you're lucky enough to find yourself stranded on a desert island with a stream of fresh water to keep you hydrated, you may find yourself surrounded by an endless supply of water that is not fit to drink. So, how can you make salt water drinkable?

Provided you have access to some wood, or some other similarly combustible material with which to make a fire, your best bet is to purify seawater using distillation.

Boil the water in whatever vessel you can find or fashion and hold something above it to collect the water vapor that rises from it. As the steam condenses on the surface above, it will leave droplets of pure potable water. Angling your collecting device appropriately will allow these droplets to run down and into your waiting thirsty mouth - or, if you're being more civilized, your cup.

104.

HOW TO MAKE
A FIRE IN SNOW

Ironically, if you're stranded in a snowy landscape, the one thing that may well prove your salvation - a roaring fire - is the one thing it feels all but impossible to make. But with enough tools and enough resources, it's not as impossible as it might seem.

Dig out the snow down to ground level and clear a space on the rocks or vegetation below. Gather what firewood you can: you may have to dig for smaller twigs and branches, while an axe will let you hack away the frozen or damp outer surface of dead trees to access the drier, more readily combustible wood inside.

You might not have the luxury of kindling or tinder, but you can always improvise with threads pulled from an item of clothing, or a few fibers picked from the padding of a coat or sleeping back. If it's especially windy, lighting several matches at once will ensure the flame holds while you start your blaze.

If you're moving on afterwards, always ensure your fire is fully extinguished and cover the ashes with more snow before you leave.

105.

HOW TO MAKE A SLING

The point of a sling is to keep an injured arm as immobilized as possible either to prevent further injury or while the injury itself heals. Medical-grade slings are padded, comfortable, and sturdy, but when such supplies are not available, you'll have to make do with what you have.

Luckily, a sling can be made fairly easily from any sizable piece of cloth, including a torn shirt or jacket. For an adult arm, ideally, you'd be looking for something around 11 square feet in size. A blanket or pillowcase would work well here, but you may have to be more ruthless - cutting open a t-shirt along a side seam should give you ample material to work with.

Fold the cloth in half diagonally to make a triangle and slide the affected arm into the crease. Try to keep the arm at a 90° angle but listen to the patient and make sure that they are comfortable. The sling should be sized so that their fingers just protrude from the outer open end.

Tie the corners of the fabric behind the neck as securely as you can.

106.

HOW TO REPAIR
A SAIL

If you're somewhere in the middle of the ocean, noticing a tear in your sail is not a welcome development. Luckily, small tears and holes can be repaired fairly easily - though larger tears, and more permanent fixtures should always be repaired once ashore.

Sailing survival kits often include adhesive sail tape these days, but at a push, any strong adhesive tape, like duct tape, will do. Stick one length of the tape one on side of the hole to block it. On the opposite side, trim or tear away any loose threads, and attach another length of tape over the hole to form as strong a seal as possible.

If the sail is wet, the tape may not catch as easily as it should, and any further wind and rain will continue to weaken the repair. So be vigilant and continue to reattach or replace the tape if it comes undone, otherwise the tear could continue to open, rendering the sail increasingly useless.

107.

HOW TO ESCAPE BEING HUNTED BY AN ANIMAL

Precisely what to do when you find you're being hunted or pursued by an animal understandably depends on precisely what that animal is.

Some creatures, like crocodiles and alligators, you can escape by climbing a tree and waiting until the croc loses interest. With others, like black bears, it's best to turn the tables on them and make them intimidated. In some cases, it's best to run and seek shelter; in others, turning and running might be the worst thing you could do, as some animals, like tigers, are more prone to attack when they cannot see your face.

Your best bet with many wild mammals, however, is likely to disrupt the scent trail you're naturally leaving behind you. Run upwind, so that whatever is hunting you loses its scent and finds tracking you more difficult. Try to put water between you and the animal, as it will naturally disperse your scent trail too.

It's often said that polar bears are so naturally inquisitive that if you drop something, like a hat or bag, behind you, they will spend so long investigating it that you'll have time to escape. That may well be just some outdoorsmen's folklore, however, as other reports say dropping anything that carries your scent will do little except convince a bear that you're worth chasing after.

In all instances, however, the best tip is simply to avoid any kind of run-in with a predator at all. Never approach dangerous wild animals (no matter how good a picture you might want to take), especially during their breeding season. Listen to local guides and experts; the US National Park Service, for instance, tailors its advice to the individual bears that you might come across. And more importantly, be aware of where you are and respectful of the kinds of wild animals you can expect to encounter.

108.

HOW TO SMASH A WINDOW

Whether escaping a burning building or an upturned car, you may well find yourself at some point needing to break open a window.

In non-emergency situations, of course, it's best to make some prior arrangements. Applying tape to the glass will stop it from breaking into pieces. Use goggles and cover as much bare skin as you can. Place a blanket or similar covering on the floor to capture any shards of falling glass.

In an emergency, however, there's often no time to prepare, but you should still be mindful that falling broken glass may be just as dangerous as whatever peril is compelling you to break the window in the first place.

Windows are typically weaker around their corners and edges, so if you're using an implement to smash one, aim your blows there. Protect your hand by wrapping it and whatever you're using to smash the glass in fabric - a jacket or shirt will do the trick. If you have no implement at hand, remember that your legs are naturally stronger than your arms, so kicking the glass - even with both feet at once, if lying down for instance - may give you a better chance of escape.

109.

HOW TO SURVIVE IN
A FALLING ELEVATOR

No matter how many times it happens in the movies, the chances of an elevator breaking and careening down through the shaft of a building are vanishingly small. The undersides of elevators have sets of emergency brakes, and just one of the metal cables from which they are suspended is typically strong enough to support the elevator itself even if all the others are sheered through.

If, after all that, you still find yourself in a falling elevator, you can nevertheless improve your chances of survival not by sitting or jumping, despite what you may have heard, but by lying down. On impact, being prone like this will spread the force throughout your body. Your buttocks - the largest muscles in your body - and body fat are natural cushions and will absorb the impact much better than your two bony knees ever could. And lying down keeps your spine perpendicular to the floor and the source of the impact, whereas standing risks compressing your delicate vertebrae and the nerves and vessels inside.

110.

HOW TO SURVIVE
ON A DESERT ISLAND

If you find yourself stranded somewhere, your immediate priorities are fresh water, food, shelter, and escape. That's all well and good on the mainland, of course, where despite being lost you might only be a few miles from potential salvation. But if you're stranded on an isolated island - with limited resources from the outset - survival is a very different game.

Natural springs, streams, or even rainwater can all be used to supply fresh water, though if you have a ready supply of firewood, it may be best to boil the water first to kill off any potentially harmful bacteria.

Finding food on an island will likely involve foraging for fruits and tubers or hunting for game or fish. You'll need to establish your best hunting techniques, and fashion your best hunters' weaponry from whatever you have available.

If resources are truly limited, you may have to fashion a shelter out of driftwood or even resort to finding a natural shelter in a cave beneath an outcrop. Either way, you can still use leaves, fern fronds, and branches to make your shelter waterproof or seal its entrance to the elements.

To escape, you can either brave the open sea in a makeshift raft or canoe or else signal for help - the best method of which will likely be to light a beacon fire on the highest point you can find.

(Check elsewhere in this book for tips on everything from canoe-carving to lighting fires with little equipment.)

111.

HOW TO PRESERVE MEAT IN THE WILD

If you're stranded and in for a long stay in the wilderness, securing a long-term supply of food may well involve preserving whatever meat Mother Nature has to offer. Luckily for you, there are a handful of different techniques that you can use, including smoking, curing, pickling, and drying.

Cut the meat into thin strips and boil it to kill off any harmful bacteria. Place the meat in direct sunlight - either by draping it over twigs or poles or on rocks - to dehydrate it naturally in the heat. The meat will become tight and sticky, like jerky, as it dries but will keep in this state for several weeks.

Boiling salt water will leave behind a supply of salt that you can use to cure meat in small quantities too. Rub the salt onto thin strips of meat and leave them to air dry.

So long as you have a supply of dry hardwood for burning (as softwood and green wood can coat your food in unpalatable and even dangerous chemicals), you can smoke your meat above a fire too. Create a canopy over the flames to keep the smoke around the strips of meat as long as possible. The smoke will not cook the meat but will preserve it by removing its moisture.

112.

HOW TO STOP
A RUNAWAY TRAIN

Modern trains have several different sets of brakes, and the chances of them all failing are small. But runaway trains are nevertheless a thing; accidents have been known to happen due to driver error, or when trains are travelling at too great a speed for the brakes to apply sufficient force to slow them down in time. So, how could you stop a runaway train?

In very simple terms, most trains have several backup systems that could be used in an emergency. So-called dynamic brakes divert energy away from the wheels (and begin using it to generate electricity instead) allowing the train to slow to a halt. Block brakes are metal clamps that can be fastened down onto the wheels of a train, applying enough pressure to stop them from turning. These can only be used over a relatively short distance, however, before friction naturally begins to take over and wear the metal of the block down, rendering it useless.

In emergency scenarios, however, a last-ditch method is to use a derailer. Trains can be sent into a siding, where an angled director can be placed on the tracks, forcing the train to derail.

113.

HOW TO FIND
A SUITABLE CAMPSITE

Finding a suitable campsite is often easier said than done as there are a great many variables worth keeping an eye on.

Avoid slopes or inclines, as rain can easily wash your camp away. Likewise, damp ground on a hot day may be a sign that where you've chosen has poor drainage and will be apt to flood if the weather turns against you. Soft ground may make it easier to insert tent pegs, but the damp ground should be avoided as much as the ground that has been baked hard.

If you're planning on starting a fire, choose a camp in open ground with no overhanging trees or branches that might easily catch alight. You might also want to select somewhere near to a source of water, so if your fire gets out of hand, you're not faced with a long trek to find sufficient water to put it out.

114.

HOW TO MAKE
YOUR OWN ROPE

A rope is made by plaiting and interlocking innumerable individual fibers that together are far stronger than any individual thread or bunch of loose thread ever could be. And in a survival situation, that's precisely how you'll manage to make your own.

First of all, you'll need to choose whatever material you want to use. If you're unlucky enough to have limited supplies, you might have to make your own fibers from threads of loose bark, dried grasses, or reeds. These will need to be dried, separated, and either spun or plaited together to make twine from which you can build your rope.

If you have a similar filament already - thread, string, yarn, or even fishing wire or dental floss will all work in an emergency - then you can begin twining your rope without all that prior preparation. Lay lengths of your material alongside one another, divide them into two or three bunches (depending on their thickness), and use a separate thread to tie them together at one end. Then you can begin either twisting, coiling, or plaiting the bunches together to make a rope.

You can splice in new bunches of fibers as you go to make a longer rope; this will be especially necessary if you're using grasses or shorter plant fibers. Once complete, tie off the opposite end and your rope is ready to use.

115.

HOW TO LIGHT
A FLARE

Chances are you've never lit a flare in your life. Hopefully, you'll never have to. But if you find yourself in a situation where you do, what exactly do you have to do?

Of all the different kinds of emergency flares, it's a road flare you'll likely have the most use for. These bright red, dynamite-like cylinders are essentially gigantic matches, with a protective plastic cap covering the lighting end. Remove the cap and turn it over. You'll see that the outside edge of the cap will have a rough surface for striking the flare against, like the side of a matchbox.

Hold the flare in front of you and strike the tip away from you so that it catches alight. Drop the flare on the ground, some distance from your vehicle, as a signal for approaching motorists.

In an emergency , however, you may find yourself needing to use a flare gun. These work on much the same principle but strike the flare automatically before firing it trailing into the air.

116.

HOW TO CLEAN
DIRTY WATER

Your safest bet when it comes to making drinkable water from dirty water is to boil it. This will leave all the impurities behind, in whatever vessel you boiled it in, and allow you to collect the pure vapor for drinking.

Besides distillation, however, emergency kits often now include specialized drinking bottles that work to purify water as you suck it up a straw, and dissolvable tablets that when dropped into water, kill off all the harmful agents it may contain, rendering it perfectly potable in a matter of minutes. If you're heading into the wilderness, it may be well worth adding one of these ingenious devices to your emergency kit.

117.

HOW TO LAND A PLANE

The pilot of your aircraft is unconscious (or worse) and it's up to you to land the plane.

First up, take the seat and buckle in; this is very likely going to be a bumpy ride. The autopilot will likely be engaged, but you may need to level the plane if it is ascending, descending, or turning in the air. Look for a dial called the altitude indicator, which will show the pitch of the aircraft relative to the horizon. Use the controls as a joystick to level the plane gradually and gently, so that the cross line in the middle of the indicator lines up with the central guideline, which represents the horizon. Pulling the controls toward you will bring the nose of the aircraft up, and vice versa.

Check the airspeed gauge to ensure that the plane's speed is within the area marked in green; if it is losing power or going too fast, you will have to adjust it.

Communicate with air traffic control using the pilot's headset; there will likely be a TTT or touch-to-talk button that will need to be activated. They will need to know your aircraft's call sign, which will be located somewhere in the cockpit (as well as written on the outside of the craft itself). Follow their instructions to find a safe place to land and begin your descent. Pull back on the throttle to reduce the plane's speed. That should naturally cause its nose to drop slightly and begin to lower the aircraft to the ground.

As you approach the runway, lower the landing gear (if it is retractable; in smaller aircraft, it is always down), and begin to deploy the decelerating flaps located along the wings. As you approach the ground, you'll need to lift the nose of the aircraft slightly so that the rear wheels touch down first.

Larger aircraft will have reverse thrust that will help slow it down, otherwise continue to reduce the power until it is safe to gentle deploy the brakes and bring the aircraft to a stop.

118.

HOW TO SURVIVE A WOLF ATTACK

Wolves aren't typically aggressive with human beings, but wolf attacks are by no means unheard of, so to be prepared to deal with one in the wilderness is a useful skill.

If you stumble across a wolf and it sees you, back away slowly while maintaining eye contact. Walk backwards, feeling with your feet along the ground to avoid tripping up. Act calmly and do not run; wolves will easily outpace you, and your panicked reaction may be all that's needed to convince them that you are indeed prey and worth pursuing.

If approached by a wolf, act aggressively. Make any noise you can - singing, shouting, clapping your hands, and stomping your feet - to appear as intimidating as possible. Again, do not run, and do not look away. If the wolf attacks, fight back. Use anything at your disposal to injure it, including rocks, sticks, or weapons. Do not play dead but continue to counterattack. A wolf will not end its attack unless convinced that you pose a threat.

If you drive the wolf off, the attack may not be over. Get to safety as best you can - even a vehicle or climbing a tree will do - and wait for any sign of the wolf or the rest of its pack. Only once you are sure the wolf has moved on should you continue on foot.

119.

HOW TO TREAT
A SNAKE BITE

There's an old bit of outdoors lore that says you can suck the venom out of a snakebite. It's not an ideal technique, and is not recommended anymore: after all, the smallest nick or open vessel in your mouth, and that venom you've just tried to suck out of your bloodstream is still going to end up in there anyway. Instead, try this.

If you can, clean the wound with soap and fresh water and bandage it, but avoid moving the area of the bite too much as this will cause the venom to circulate more readily. If you've been bitten on an arm or a leg, for instance, keep the limb itself as still as possible.

Many snakes have enormously potent venom, which can be fatal to humans, so be acutely aware of any signs of truly dangerous envenomation, like feverishness, blurred vision, breathlessness, palpitations, and inflammation or discoloration of the bite area. Remove any tight clothing or jewelry near the bite, as any swelling may lead to these causing even further injury.

All snake bites, no matter how serious, should be assessed by medical professionals. If you've been bitten by a snake with potentially fatal venom, moreover, your only option is emergency treatment with the relevant antivenom. At the hospital, the doctors will need to know what kind of snake has bitten you, so, if possible, identify the snake or take a picture of it on your phone. Never try to capture it, pursue it, or kill it.

120.

HOW TO SURVIVE
A SHARK ATTACK

You're certainly by no means alone if you find sharks absolutely terrifying - and find the prospect of a shark attack even more frightening. But as much as we might think of sharks as unimpeachable killing machines, shark attacks are not always fatal. Indeed, a few tips and methods have been devised over the years to improve a person's chances of survival if they were to encounter one.

Sharks have several sensitive parts to their head and face, most notably their eyes, snout, and gills. If a shark has hold of you, directing blows here - not just with your hands, but with your feet, knees, elbow, or even anything you may be holding, like an underwater camera - may well cause the shark to think twice about continuing the attack. Continue fighting back for as long as you can.

So long as the shark relents, your next priority is to seek help. Shark bites are notoriously brutal, as their multiple rows of serrated teeth are designed to inflict devastating damage to their prey, so get back to shore - or to the nearest vessel - as quickly as possible before your blood loss becomes too great.

121.

HOW TO FIND YOUR
WAY OUT OF A FOREST

There's a moment in the *Blair Witch Project*, where the three filmmakers lost in the woods stumble across a stream. They've lost their map and have no idea where they are with – ahem - certain supernatural consequences.

Ironically, stumbling across a stream is the perfect solution to finding your way out of a forest. Streams flow into larger rivers, around which, for obvious reasons, we humans have built settlements since time immemorial. Following a stream will therefore very likely take you back to a civilization of some description.

When you're truly lost, however, the woods can be a devastatingly disorientating place to be. One direction looks exactly like the other, and as much as you might try to walk in a straight line, with trees and undergrowth to walk around, you might very easily find yourself drifting off and circling back on yourself. Luckily, there's a simple hack to avoid that.

Find yourself a long straight pole or branch. Hold that straight out in front of you and drop it to the ground. The branch won't mind being passed through forks in trees, pushed through dense undergrowth, and or even jostled through thorn bushes - in fact, it can go dead straight ahead in all the places you can't.

Once it's on the forest floor, walk to the other end and do the same again. No matter how much of a detour you may need to make to reach the end of the stick, the stick itself will stay straight and true.

Essentially, you'll be making a path through the forest without actually making a path. Following the straight line forward should eventually lead you out of the woods and from there allow you to get your bearings once more.

122.

HOW TO BUILD
A MAKESHIFT WEAPON

We've dealt with slingshots, fishing spikes, and bows and arrows already in this book, but they're not the only weapons you might be able to fashion in the wild.

Fastening or binding a rock into the cleft of a Y-shaped branch is a simple means of making a weighted club, or if the rock is sharp enough, an axe. Horns, bones, or discarded antlers are all, natural weaponry too, and if necessary, can be fastened to the ends of shafts to make spears.

Makeshift twine can be used to make snares and tripwires, and lining a camouflaged pit with sharpened posts is an easy way to make a pit trap.

123.

HOW TO SEE OFF
A CHARGING ANIMAL

If a large animal charges at you - as enraged elephants, hippos, rhinos, and bears are all prone to doing - the short answer, unsurprisingly, is that you should run.

Some animals will only perform so-called "dummy" charges, meant to intimidate, in which case speeding away in the opposite direction as quickly should be enough to see off the attack. If the charge is more determined, however, your response needs to be immediate and assured, depending on the creature.

With bears, standing your ground and intimidating the bear as much as it intimidates you - by shouting, clapping, and stamping your feet - should spook it enough to see it off. Elephants, rhinos, and hippos, however, are more determined and are more likely to see through a charge regardless of how intimidating that you may try to be.

Your best response here is to run in a zigzag, as you'll be able to turn more sharply than it will because of its sheer size. Then hide out of sight - behind a rock, up a tree, or ideally, in a vehicle. Continue putting distance between you and the animal until the threat is over.

124.

HOW TO SURVIVE
A SHIPWRECK

If you're on a vessel that's sinking at sea, seek your nearest personal flotation device, or PFD, and put it on.

Larger ships will have evacuation alarms and procedures, in which case - much like leaving an aircraft in an emergency - follow the advice and the orders of the crew, which will likely involve making your way to a life raft. Smaller vessels, including your own, will obviously have different protocols, but if it becomes obvious the ship is lost, you need to be prepared to abandon it.

If you have to jump into the water, the ship may well be listing, in which case leap from the side closest to the water's surface to shorten your jump and lower the chance of injury. Once in the water, swim to the nearest lifeboat, or as far away from the sinking ship as possible so as not to get pulled down when it finally sinks below the waves.

Ideally, a mayday signal will have already been called, in which case - regardless of whether you're in the water or on a life raft - you need only await rescue.

125.

HOW TO BREAK DOWN A DOOR

To kick or break down a door, first double-check where and on what side the hinges are located. That will understandably be the stronger side, so you'll want to aim your blows toward the opposite edge.

Doors are typically weakest where the locks are mounted, so kick against the door either just above or just below the locking mechanism. Alternatively, aim for the corners, or nearest to the latch.

To create maximum power against the door, stand around a leg's length away from the door. Kick with your dominant foot while planting the heel of your other foot firmly into the ground. Kick with the sole of your foot flat against the door, but keep your knee slightly bent to absorb the impact. Continue until the door swings open or the wood splinters enough to clamber through.

126.

HOW TO SURVIVE
A WILDFIRE

If you're caught out by a wildfire, escape on foot is difficult but by no means impossible.

Keep low to the ground where the air will be clearer. To reduce smoke inhalation, pull your clothing up over your mouth and nose, ideally dampening it with water. If the fire gets too close, switch to a dry cloth to cover your nose, as the fire can evaporate the water and damage your airways even more.

The most dangerous places to be are uphill from the flames and downwind from the fire. If you are far enough away from the fire, monitor its movement as best you can and always try to remain upwind of it. If the wind is blowing past you and toward the fire, run into the wind. If the wind is behind the fire and blowing it and its flames toward you, run crossways, perpendicular to the fire.

If possible, head for non-flammable land. That may include parking lots or large open concrete spaces, or even land that has already been burned. If there is a stream or watercourse nearby, try to put it between you and the fire.

If the fire catches up with you or surrounds you, you may have to hunker down and see it out. Find a low spot, preferably with no overhanging trees or vegetation. Drag a layer or mud or earth over yourself - anything that can provide some protection between the heat of the flames. Keep your head down, lying on your belly, and remain in place until the fire passes.

127.

HOW TO FIND FOOD
IN THE WILD

Finding food in the wild depends on where exactly you are and what time of year it is.

Catching fish, for instance, becomes a lot harder and more dangerous during the winter months when lakes and rivers are iced over. In which case, foraging for a more vegetarian diet - or switching your technique to snaring game, like grouse or rabbits - might be a better option.

Your food options will be limited by the equipment at your disposal too. If you're in the wilderness with a trusty kit bag or are stranded with tools or even weapons, your options will be different from if you're stranded with nothing.

Be wary too of foods and creatures that may be poisonous or venomous. If in doubt, you're better off not taking the risk, but with few other options, you may be left with no choice.

Check elsewhere in this book for tips on hunting, foraging, and ascertaining just how safe something is to eat.

128.

HOW TO SURVIVE
A SNOWSTORM

Seeing out a blizzard depends on how long the storm is forecast to last (given enough prior warning, you may find it necessary to shop for supplies), and where exactly you are (hunkering down at home is obviously going to be more comfortable than being trapped in your car).

If you're at home, keep abreast of the weather reports, and keep yourself as calm and as comfortable as possible. Stay in touch with your family, friends, and neighbors and keep yourself as healthy as possible - eating well and drinking plenty of water - so that when the storm abates, you're fit enough to get back outside as soon as possible.

If you're trapped outdoors, seek shelter as soon as possible - even if that shelter is your car. In your vehicle, other than to ensure your exhaust pipe is free of snow, remain inside at all times. Provided you have enough fuel, run your engine for 10–20 minutes every so often to use the heaters, charge your phone, and check in with the weather forecast. Keep your body and brain active, and despite being inside, keep moving as and when you can to keep your blood circulating. Clapping your hands and tapping your feet will keep you focused and warm. If you have a winter survival kit, you may well be prepped with food, blankets, and even hot water; otherwise, make do with what you have and await rescue.

CONCLUSION

The odd thing about a book like this is that, hopefully, you'll never need anything that's inside it. Hopefully, you'll never be dummy charged by a rhino or find yourself in a situation where you're trying to start a file with a battery in a snowstorm.

Hopefully, you'll never be on a sinking ship, compelled to identify the snake that has bitten you, or forced to work out where the nearest high land is to escape an incoming tsunami.

And hopefully, you'll certainly never have to recall how to wrap up your own severed limb, or perform your own invasive abdominal surgery…

Such is the way of the world, however, that we never know quite what's around the corner, and so – hopefully - the hints and survival tips outlined in this book may indeed come in useful.